National System Planning for Protected Areas

IUCN – The World Conservation Union

Founded in 1948, The World Conservation Union brings together States, government agencies and a diverse range of non-governmental organizations in a unique world partnership: over 895 members in all, spread across some 137 countries.

As a Union, IUCN seeks to influence, encourage and assist societies throughout the world to conserve the integrity and diversity of nature and to ensure that any use of natural resources is equitable and ecologically sustainable. A central secretariat coordinates the IUCN Programme and serves the Union membership, representing their views on the world stage and providing them with the strategies, services, scientific knowledge and technical support they need to achieve their goals. Through its six Commissions, IUCN draws together over 6000 expert volunteers in project teams and action groups, focusing in particular on species and biodiversity conservation and the management of habitats and natural resources. The Union has helped many countries to prepare National Conservation Strategies, and demonstrates the application of its knowledge through the field projects it supervises. Operations are increasingly decentralized and are carried forward by an expanding network of regional and country offices, located principally in developing countries.

The World Conservation Union builds on the strengths of its members, networks and partners to enhance their capacity and to support global alliances to safeguard natural resources at local, regional and global levels.

Cardiff University

The Department of City and Regional Planning, Cardiff University is pleased to be a partner in the production of this important series of guidelines for protected area planning and management. The Department, through its Environmental Planning Research Unit, is actively involved in protected areas research; runs specialised courses on planning and environmental policy; and has a large Graduate School offering opportunities for persons interested in pursuing research for a PhD or as part of wider career development. If you are interested in learning more about the Department, its research capabilities and courses please write to us at the address given below.

Professor Jeremy Alden BSc M.Litt PhD MRTPI
Head of Department
Department of City and Regional Planning
Cardiff University
PO BOX 906
Cardiff
CF1 3YN

Tel: ++ 44 1222 874308
Fax: ++ 44 1222 874845
Email: AldenJD@cf.ac.uk

National System Planning for Protected Areas

Main Author: Adrian G. Davey
Applied Ecology Research Group
Faculty of Applied Science, University of Canberra
P.O. Box 1 Belconnen ACT, Australia

Series Editor: Adrian Phillips

World Commission on Protected Areas (WCPA)

Best Practice Protected Area Guidelines Series No. 1

IUCN – The World Conservation Union
1998

This publication has been made possible to a large part by funding from Cardiff University. Additional funding has been graciously provided by the Government of Norway, Directorate for Nature Management, National Park Division.

Published by: IUCN, Gland, Switzerland, and Cambridge, UK.

Citation: Davey, A.G. (1998). *National System Planning for Protected Areas*. IUCN, Gland, Switzerland and Cambridge, UK. x + 71pp.

ISBN: 2-8317-0399-9

Cover design by: IUCN Publications Services Unit

Cover photo: Isla Culebra National Wildlife Refuge (IUCN Category IV), Puerto Rico. *Pedro Rosabal*

Layout by: IUCN Publications Services Unit

Produced by: IUCN Publications Services Unit, Cambridge, UK

Printed by: Page Bros (Norwich) Ltd, UK

Available from: IUCN Publications Services Unit
219c Huntingdon Road, Cambridge CB3 ODL,
United Kingdom
Tel: ++44 1223 277894
Fax: ++44 1223 277175
E-mail: iucn-psu@wcmc.org.uk
http://www.iucn.org
A catalogue of IUCN publications is also available

The text of this book is printed on 90gsm Fineblade Cartridge made from low-chlorine pulp.

Contents

Editorial preface

This is the first in a new series of Best Practice Guidelines produced by the IUCN World Commission on Protected Areas (WCPA) in partnership with the Environmental Planning Research Unit, Department of City and Regional Planning, University of Wales, Cardiff, UK.

WCPA, which is an integral part of IUCN – the World Conservation Union, is a world-wide network of some 1,300 protected areas experts. Its members work in a volunteer capacity to raise the standard of protected areas planning and management. The Department of City and Regional Planning at the University of Wales is the UK's leading school of planning. It has a strong international reputation and a high profile in research and teaching related to environmental topics. Together the two bodies are working to produce and distribute a series of world best practice guidelines. There will be two publications a year, prepared through experts drawn from WCPA's network, initially over a three year period. Drafting of each individual guideline publication will be led by a main author, usually assisted by a task force and subject to peer review within WCPA. The series will address key issues facing protected areas around the world: future guidelines will deal with topics such as the economic benefits of protected areas, marine protected areas, tourism and protected areas, financing of protected areas, and training.

The guidelines series is intended to be used by all those concerned with the policy and practice of protected areas, not only the practitioners but also decision-makers at the various levels of government, others such as NGOs and academics, and international funding agencies. Through the publication and distribution of these guidelines, WCPA and Cardiff hope to improve understanding of the needs of protected areas management and the standards of management on the ground.

As series editor, I welcome feed-back from readers.

Adrian Phillips
Chair WCPA and Professor of Countryside
and Environmental Planning at the Department of
City and Regional Planning, University of Wales, Cardiff, UK.

Acknowledgements

These guidelines were compiled by Adrian Davey of the University of Canberra, Australia, with extensive input from a project steering committee consisting of Bruce Amos (Parks Canada), John Hough (UNDP), Kathy Mackinnon (World Bank), Lota Melamari (Tanzania National Parks), Pedro Rosabal (IUCN), David Sheppard (IUCN) and George Stankey (Oregon State University). Jeffrey McNeely (IUCN), Adrian Phillips (WCPA), Murray McComb (Parks Canada), Stuart Chape and Clive Marsh (IUCN Lao PDR), Bruce Davis (WCPA) and Larry Hamilton (WCPA) also made valuable contributions.

Foreword

Protected areas are essential for the conservation of biological diversity and for meeting a range of community objectives. World-wide, there is a current growth in protected areas: both the number of sites and the area under protection have increased substantially over recent decades. But ensuring that appropriate management is in place to realise the potential benefits remains a major problem in many places.

Co-ordination is undertaken at the international level by organisations such as IUCN – The World Conservation Union – particularly its World Commission on Protected Areas (WCPA) (Formerly the IUCN Commission on National Parks and Protected Areas – CNPPA). However, the greatest need is to secure the integrity and effective management of protected areas at the national level. These guidelines outline key issues which need to be addressed in national level planning for a system of protected areas.

A system plan is the design of a total reserve system covering the full range of ecosystems and communities found in a particular country. The plan should identify the range of purposes of protected areas, and help to balance different objectives. The plan should also identify the relationships among the system components – between individual areas, between protected areas and other land uses, and between different sectors and levels of the society concerned. It should help demonstrate important linkages with other aspects of economic development, and show how various stakeholders can interact and co-operate to support effective and sustainable management of protected areas. Lastly, a system plan should be a means to establish the priorities for a workable national system of protected areas.

These guidelines identify links between system planning and the Convention on Biological Diversity and are intended to be used by governments and others in the implementation of Article 8 of the Convention, (*In situ* conservation). The guidance is also set in the context of the range of protected area management categories which have recently been adopted by IUCN. The guidelines emphasise that judgement is required – to ask relevant questions, to understand driving influences and to make choices about the level of detail and strategic orientation of a system plan relevant to the prevailing circumstances of a country. Because countries vary greatly in terms of their physical, economic and social conditions, advice of this kind must be general: accordingly these guidelines provide a broad framework for system planning at the national level, rather than seeking to answer every question or issue which might arise at that level.

Abbreviations and acronyms

CITES	Convention on International Trade in Endangered Species of Wild Flora and Fauna
CNPPA	[former] Commission on National Parks and Protected Areas of IUCN – now the World Commission on Protected Areas (WCPA)
GEF	Global Environment Facility
IUCN	The World Conservation Union (International Union for Conservation of Nature and Natural Resources)
NGO	Non-governmental organisation
Ramsar	Convention on Wetlands of International Importance especially as Waterfowl Habitat
UN	United Nations
UNEP	United Nations Environment Programme
UNESCO	United Nations Educational, Scientific and Cultural Organisation
WCMC	World Conservation Monitoring Centre
WCPA	World Commission on Protected Areas of IUCN
WWF	World Wide Fund for Nature

1. Introduction

1.1 Scope and objectives of the guidelines

A guideline is a clear statement, based on *best* available knowledge, which provides guidance in relation to a particular issue. This document is designed to provide such statements to assist the planning of a national system of protected areas. However, because the relevance of issues is context-dependent and the circumstances of countries are so varied, the guidelines are not presented as "rules". Rather, they provide an overview of the issues which need to be addressed and discuss some of the options for their resolution. The aim is to encourage the reader to ask questions, rather than provide a "cook book" approach to developing a system plan.

These guidelines have been written for several audiences:

1. Decision makers who work in protected area agencies, both government and non-government, at the international, national, regional or local level;

2. Decision makers and stakeholders who are indirectly involved with (or whose actions influence) protected areas, also at various levels;

3. Funding agencies and other investors; and

4. Protected area practitioners and WCPA members world-wide.

Because the target audience is so wide, these guidelines have been oriented at the policy rather than the operational level, and assume prior knowledge of what protected areas are and why they are necessary.

The guidelines build on the extensive literature referred to in the next section and incorporate the outcomes of meetings convened by IUCN and WCPA, and their partners, in many parts of the world since the Fourth World Parks Congress in Caracas in 1992. The guidance has been kept as short and succinct as possible, and has been organised with a view to later evaluation and further development.

1.2 Protected areas, the Convention on Biological Diversity and system plans

IUCN has defined a protected area as the following:

Box 1. Definition of protected areas

"an area of land and/or sea especially dedicated to the protection and maintenance of biological diversity, and of natural and associated cultural resources, and managed through legal or other effective means" (IUCN 1994a).

There are now over 30,300 protected areas, totalling well over 13.2 million hectares covering 8.84% of the world's land area (Green and Paine, 1997). Both number and area have expanded greatly in recent decades – about two thirds of the protected areas having been established within the last 30 years. Over the same period there has also been a significant increase in the number of countries with protected areas. These trends reflect accelerating and widespread concern for conservation and the growing political significance of environmental issues, a concern which also led to the signing of the Convention on Biological Diversity in 1992.

In general, this rapid and recent growth in protected areas (see Map 1) has not been accompanied by commensurate expansion in management capacity. Allocation of land and/or water to protected status has often not resolved (and in some cases has heightened) conflicts over access, use or control of the areas concerned. Economic recession and hardship have thrown such issues into sharper focus in recent years.

Protected areas will not survive unless they enjoy broad public support and this will not exist unless people's fundamental needs are met. Land use and resource management conflicts, inequities or impacts do not go away simply because an area is given protected status. When they are established by nation states or related entities, protected area boundaries often reflect considerations of sovereignty, governance and tenure as much as the environment types they seek to protect. For all these reasons, the planning and management of protected areas must be co-ordinated with the use and management of other areas rather than treated in isolation. The long term success of protected areas must be seen in the light of the search for more sustainable patterns of development in general.

System planning offers a more practical way of putting protected areas management into this wider context.

Protected area system plans are called for under Article 8 of the Convention on Biological Diversity (Glowka *et al.*,1994), in which protected areas are identified as having an important role in the conservation of biodiversity. The specific requirements of the Convention are set out in Box 2.

Box 2. Specific requirements relating to protected areas in the Convention on Biological Diversity; articles 8(a) and (b)

"(a)   Establish a system of protected areas or areas where special measures need to be taken to conserve biological diversity;

(b)   Develop, where necessary, guidelines for the selection, establishment and management of protected areas where special measures need to be taken to conserve biological diversity;"

Thus, governments have now agreed a clear mandate under the Convention for coordinated protected area planning at the national level. The system plan is a means of carrying this out, for protected areas also serve many functions other than biodiversity conservation. It is essential that protected area system planning be integrated with

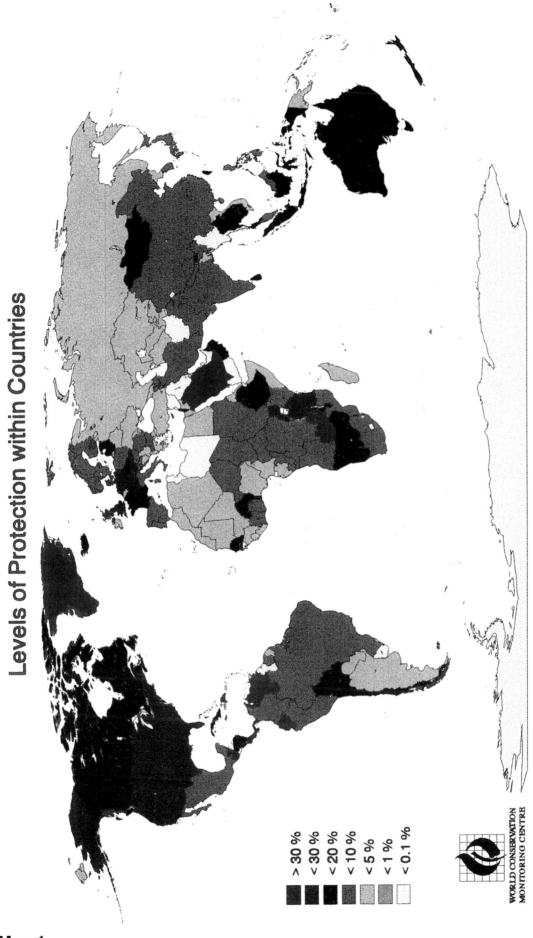

Map 1

national biodiversity strategies, national conservation strategies, ecologically sustainable development strategies and other national-level planning (e.g. Nelson 1987).

The Caracas Action Plan (IUCN 1992a, McNeely 1993) adopted at the Fourth World Parks Congress also identified national protected area system plans as a priority (see Box 3).

Box 3. Requirements of the Caracas Action Plan relating to national system plans for protected areas

"Action 1.1-Develop and implement national protected area system plans. Develop national system plans as the primary national policy document for strengthening management and extending protected area coverage. Base state or provincial plans on the national plan.

Identify all the groups with a particular interest in protected areas and enable them to participate actively in the system planning process. Review the system plan widely with all potential interest groups and agencies before final adoption, and periodically thereafter.

Mobilise the best available science to identify critical sites that need to be included in the system if the nation's full range of biodiversity is to be protected, and to provide guidance on appropriate management policies for the individual sites and their surrounding lands.

Include within the system a range of terrestrial and marine protected area categories that addresses the needs of all interest groups, including agriculture, forestry, and fisheries. Ensure that all sites managed for conservation objectives are incorporated, including tribal lands, forest sanctuaries, and other sites managed by agencies other than the main protected areas management authority (for example, private landowners, local communities, and the military)."

Although there is no one model which is universally appropriate, a number of countries have developed system plans in recent years. Examples include Canada (Canada, Environment Canada 1991; see also Appendix 3.1), the Dominican Republic (Republica Dominicana. DVS 1990), India (Rodgers and Panwar 1988), Laos (Salter and Phanthavong 1989; see also Appendix 3.2), Saudi Arabia (Child and Grainger 1990), Venezuela (Venezuela, MARNR 1989) and Western Samoa (Pearsall and Whistler 1991). System planning does have an extensive body of knowledge and field experience on which to build (Hart 1966, Forster 1973, Mackinnon *et al.*, 1986, Thorsell 1990, Kelleher and Kenchington 1991, McNeely and Thorsell 1991, Harrison 1992, Lucas 1992, Poore 1992, Harmon 1994, IUCN 1994a), as well as an extensive technical literature in conservation biology and conservation evaluation.

The core idea of protected area system planning is simple enough – that effective planning and management of protected areas requires a co-ordinated approach, both with respect to the various units within the system, and with other land uses and management activities.

1.3 The IUCN protected area management categories

In the light of experience, and the new definition of protected areas (IUCN 1994a), the IUCN scheme of graded protected area types has been revised and simplified by WCPA into six categories according to their primary management objectives (IUCN 1994) (see Box 4).

Box 4. IUCN Protected Area Management Categories

I.   Strict protection:

    a)   Strict Nature Reserve;

    b)   Wilderness Area.

II.   Ecosystem conservation and recreation (National Park).

III. Conservation of natural features (Natural Monument).

IV. Conservation through active management (Habitat/Species Management Area).

V.   Landscape/seascape conservation and recreation (Protected Landscape/ Seascape.

VI. Sustainable use of natural ecosystems (Managed Resource Protected Area).

Further details of these categories are given in Appendix 2. The classification scheme can be used both normatively and descriptively – to outline the way in which sites in each class should be managed, and to provide a descriptive classification for sites already managed in a particular way.

To date, this second, descriptive approach has been more commonly used. However, while most countries have some areas within at least a few of these categories, very few, if any, are taking full advantage of the *entire* range of categories to ensure that conservation efforts are most effectively implemented (see Table 1). The IUCN protected area management categories thus provide an opportunity for a fresh look at what protected areas can achieve in all countries.

Table 1. Number and extent of protected areas within each WCPA region, classified by IUCN management category

Source: Green, M.J.B. and Paine, J.R. (1997).

WCPA region / Area of region (km²)	Ia No.	Ia Extent (km²)	Ia % of PA	Ib No.	Ib Extent (km²)	Ib %¹ of PA	II No.	II Extent (km²)	II %¹ of PA	III No.	III Extent (km²)	III %¹ of PA	IV No.	IV Extent (km²)	IV %¹ of PA	V No.	V Extent (km²)	V %¹ of PA	VI No.	VI Extent (km²)	VI %¹ of PA	I–VI No.	I–VI Extent (km²)	I–VI %
North Africa/Middle East 12,866,541	30	1,706	0.16	3	32	0.003	60	123,673	11.92	39	12,265	1.18	264	69,836	6.73	125	52,056	5.02	21	778,010	74.98	542	1,037,578	8.06
Europe 5,061,153	516	77,612	12.86	77	6,781	1.12	215	80,509	13.34	457	1,610	0.27	5,330	84,218	13.9	2,654	339,765	56.3	76	12,976	2.15	9,335	603,471	11.92
Antarctic 14,268,633	82	3,174	83.75	0		0.00	2	146	3.85	0	0	0.00	14	460	12.14	1	10	0.26	0	0	0.00	99	3,790	0.03
Pacific 555,140	27	856	6.52	0	0	0.00	11	253	1.92	19	282	2.15	50	1,072	8.12	11	48	0.37	34	10,618	80.87	152	13,129	2.37
Caribbean 238,627	20	1,078	1.0	0	0	0.00	67	12,098	11.12	22	28	0.03	231	78,989	72.61	60	14,985	13.77	177	1,605	1.48	577	108,783	45.59
North America 23,443,386	661	58,711	1.44	630	391,914	9.6	1,286	1,633,642	39.9	342	58,472	1.43	1,249	822,686	20.12	2,085	245,301	6.0	461	877,053	21.45	6,714	4,087,779	17.44
Australia/New Zealand 7,947,450	2,184	248,447	22.4	61	40,074	3.61	685	266,109	24.0	940	7,492	0.67	1,636	10,798	0.97	65	59,856	5.4	311	476,249	42.94	5,882	1,109,025	13.95
North Eurasia 22,100,900	173	321,410	48.85	1	635	0.1	55	101,342	15.4	30	105	0.02	368	233,968	35.56	21	482	0.07	0	0	0.00	648	657,942	2.98
South-East Asia 4,498,111	293	27,832	5.36	0	0	0.00	150	190,473	36.7	62	3,944	0.76	151	91,729	17.68	109	20,491	3.95	759	184,397	35.54	1,524	518,866	11.54
South Asia 4,368,713	33	3,398	1.6	0	0	0.00	108	62,994	29.58	1	0	0.00	564	143,200	67.25	9	1,562	0.73	4	1,771	0.83	719	212,925	4.87
East Asia 11,790,494	57	90,732	10.27	24	498,673	56.43	56	74,434	8.42	73	11,382	1.29	306	63,730	7.21	159	60,719	6.87	403	84,012	9.51	1,078	883,682	7.49
South America 18,001,095	253	106,835	5.81	1	1,000	0.05	360	619,788	33.7	75	83,726	4.55	197	229,382	12.47	245	250,138	13.6	306	547,960	29.8	1,437	1,838,829	10.22
Central America 542,750	26	11,431	13.28	0	0	0.00	78	29,383	34.15	27	9,591	11.14	163	14,150	16.44	9	54	0.06	81	21,441	24.91	384	86,050	15.85
Africa (Western/Central) 13,352,849	33	28,577	3.79	5	150	0.02	82	305,268	40.46	3	4,007	0.53	175	358,415	47.5	1	100	0.01	52	57,925	7.67	351	754,442	5.65
Africa (Eastern/Southern) 10,773,580	7	688	0.05	4	1,085	0.08	168	501,351	37.98	32	118	0.01	471	257,476	19.5	25	11,883	0.9	212	547,430	41.47	919	1,320,032	12.25
Total 149,809,422	4,395	982,487	7.42	806	940,344	7.1	3,383	4,001,463	30.23	2,122	193,022	1.46	11,169	2,460,110	18.58	5,578	1,057,450	7.99	2,897	3,601,447	27.21	30,350	13,236,324	8.84

¹ Area in IUCN management category as a percentage of total area protected in region.
² Total area protected in region (all categories) as a percentage of total area in region.

6

Galapagos National Park (Category II) and Natural World Heritage Site, Ecuador.

Machu Pichu Historic Sanctuary (Category II) and World Heritage Site, Peru.

Tatra National Park (Category II) and Biosphere Reserve in Poland.

Canaima National Park (Category II) and World Heritage Site, Venezuela.

Lanin National Park (Category II), Argentina.

The Great National Park Sierra Maestra (Category VI) include a number of different protected areas under different management categories and allow productive zones for the use of natural resources, which mainly include forestry, coffee plantations, tourism and recreation.

Los Haitises National Park (Category II), in the Dominican Republic.

Okskiy Zapovednik (Category I) in Russia.

2. System planning

2.1 What is system planning?

In a general sense, system planning is an organised approach to macro-level planning. It is not a new concept, but builds on existing knowledge and approaches. System planning is a framework for understanding and using systems ideas. It is also a vehicle for convincing others. It is much more than data gathering. It must be a dynamic process. It is a means, not an end. Box 5 lists the main uses to which a system plan can be put.

Box 5. The uses of a national system plan for protected areas

- clarifying objectives;

- promoting achievement of objectives;

- identifying options and their implications;

- encouraging systematic evaluation of options;

- increasing understanding of issues;

- defining of future management issues;

- predicting and orienting future actions;

- identifying priorities for investment;

- co-ordinating a range of inputs;

- building and sustaining commitment;

- creating and maintaining partnerships; and

- establishing a baseline for evaluating future action, and for monitoring.

When system planning is applied to protected areas, it aims to maximise the desirable characteristics of a national protected area system. This should be done in a way which recognises prevailing conditions in each country arising from its environmental inheritance, history, social, political, economic and cultural context.

In relation to protected areas, system planning is about:

- defining the priority of protected areas as a worthwhile national concern; defining the relationships between (a) different units and categories of protected areas; and (b) protected areas and other relevant categories of land;

9

■ taking a more strategic view of protected areas;

■ defining roles of key players in relation to protected areas and the relationships between these players; this may include building support and a constituency for protected areas (i.e. as a means to that end, not as an end in itself);

■ identifying gaps in protected area coverage (including opportunities and needs for connectivity) and deficiencies in management; and

■ identifying current and potential impacts – both those affecting protected areas from surrounding lands and those emanating from the protected areas which affect surrounding lands.

A system plan is a statement and a set of ideas. It will usually be in one or more documents, and should incorporate maps and relevant background information. It has descriptive and strategic elements – characterising the present and charting a pragmatic way forward to a clearly stated future. The plan should provide guidance on mechanisms, institutions and procedures for co-ordinating protected areas with other aspects of land use and social development in the country concerned. It must identify relevant means of co-ordination between central and decentralised levels, and between different regions and individual protected areas. It should describe current and proposed protected areas, their condition and the management challenge which they present. It may also need to identify the mandate for, or argue the legitimacy of, protected areas as a priority concern in the context of that country. It should spell out the responsibilities and processes for developing, funding and managing the system and for co-ordinating its components.

2.2 Why system planning?

The major threats to conservation in most countries lie outside the protected area system. Unless the linkages between protected area management and external factors are identified and addressed, fundamental conservation issues are difficult to resolve. Protected area system plans cannot therefore focus solely on protected areas, but must address broader issues of concern to society. The reasons for taking a systems approach to planning are listed in Box 6.

A system approach improves the probability of substantial progress in conservation. It also promotes a truly integrated approach to linking conservation with other human endeavours.

A system plan will not of itself remove obstacles to progress in biodiversity conservation, community development or protected area management, but if the key issues have been addressed in an appropriate way it should facilitate their removal and should help clearly identify the priorities. A plan cannot create an effective protected area system overnight, nor can it produce immediate change in factors which may be compromising conservation status or management performance. It is, however, a potentially powerful tool and an essential step in achieving these ends.

Box 6. The reasons for adopting a system approach

- to relate protected areas to national priorities, and to prioritise different aspects of protected area development;

- to facilitate access to international and national funding, by defining priorities for investment in protected areas and increasing the level of confidence in the efficient use of funds and resources;

- to get away from a case by case, *ad hoc*, approach to resource management decision making;

- to target proposed additions to the protected area estate in a more rational and persuasive manner than *ad hoc* planning;

- to facilitate integration with other relevant planning strategies, such as those for national tourism, national biodiversity conservation or sustainable development;

- to help resolve conflicts, assist in making decisions relating to trade-offs, clarify roles and responsibilities of different stakeholders, and facilitate diverse stakeholder involvement;

- to provide a broader perspective for addressing site-specific issues, such as tourism management;

- to enhance the effectiveness and efficiency of the way in which budgets are developed and spent;

- to assist in meeting obligations under international treaties;

- to assist countries to be more proactive in conservation management, and in developing effective protected area systems;

- to encourage consideration of a "system" which incorporates formal protected areas and areas outside of protected areas;

- to provide a structured framework for a system of protected areas, ranging from areas managed for strict conservation to areas managed for a range of conservation and appropriate ecologically-sound activities;

- to assist protected area agencies to build political support for protected areas as a worthwhile concern;

- to define a better process of decentralisation and regionalization of protected area activities, resources and responsibilities, including the involvement of NGOs and the private sector; and

- to foster transboundary collaboration (see e.g. Thorsell 1990).

Box 7 lists some of the factors which might to lead to an ineffective or unworkable system plan.

Box 7. Some reasons why national system plans for protected areas fail

- they do not specify assumptions, rationale and criteria;

- they do not address key issues;

- they fail to involve stakeholders;

- they cover issues in too much detail;

- they cover too many areas and issues;

- they rely too much on "external experts" and fail to involve local people;

- they are weak on implementation;

- they fail to raise political support for protected areas as a worthwhile concern;

- they are poorly publicised;

- they are overambitious and ignore budget constraints; and

- they rely too much on external support and/or funding.

3. Protected area systems

3.1 Characteristics of a system

Protected areas are a key part of *in situ* conservation under the Convention on Biological Diversity, but no protected area will succeed if managed in isolation. There are biological, social and economic connections between different places and different system components; moreover, the processes of interaction are complex and dynamic. By switching the focus from individual protected areas to looking at the relationships between them, and putting the whole protected area network into its broader context, system planning provides the means for ensuring that the total significance and effectiveness of a national protected areas system is much more than the sum of the parts.

There are at least five key characteristics (discussed in section 3.1.1 to 3.1.5) of a system of protected areas:

- representativeness, comprehensiveness and balance;

- adequacy;

- coherence and complementarity;

- consistency; and

- cost effectiveness, efficiency and equity.

While these characteristics define a system overall, they also serve as criteria against which individual areas can be assessed for their potential or actual contribution to the system relative to other areas. The balance between the criteria is unavoidably subjective and dependent on the circumstances of each country. The criteria are closely linked and cannot be considered in isolation from one another. In applying these criteria, and selecting system components, consideration should be given to questions of irreplaceability and flexibility.

3.1.1 Representativeness, comprehensiveness and balance

Including highest quality examples of the full range of environment types within a country; includes the extent to which protected areas provide balanced sampling of the environment types they purport to represent.

This applies particularly to the biodiversity of the country (at relevant levels, such as genetic, species and habitat), but should also apply to other features such as landform types and to cultural landscapes. Since it is most unlikely that any one protected area could be representative of the full range of biogeographic diversity within a single country, representativeness will nearly always require the development of a network of individual protected areas.

In some parts of the world, existing protected area systems give too much attention to charismatic fauna, or spectacular scenery, and not enough to covering the full suite of plant and animal species which are characteristic of particular ecological zones.

Often existing protected areas do not sample biodiversity in any systematic way, having been created in an *ad hoc*, opportunistic fashion. In many countries, there appears to be a need for fresh surveys to identify the environment types and biodiversity at the national level, with a view to re-designing protected areas, so as to maximise representation of biodiversity and of natural and related cultural landscapes (see Table 2).

Table 2. Extent and protection of the world's major biomes
Source: Green, M.J.B. and Paine, J.R. (1997).

Biome		Protected Area		
Name	Area (km^2)	Number	Extent (km^2)	% Biome Protected
Tropical humid forests	10,513,210	1,030	922,453	8.77%
Subtropical/temperate rain forests/ woodlands	3,930,979	977	404,497	10.29%
Temperate needle-leaf forests/ woodlands	15,682,817	1,492	897,375	5.72%
Tropical dry forests/woodlands	17,312,538	1,290	1,224,566	7.07%
Temperate broad-leaf forests	11,216,659	3,905	403,298	3.60%
Evergreen sclerophyllous forests	3,757,144	1,469	164,883	4.39%
Warm deserts/semi-deserts	24,279,843	605	1,173,025	4.83%
Cold-winter deserts	9,250,252	290	546,168	5.90%
Tundra communities	22,017,390	171	1,845,188	8.38%
Tropical grasslands/savannas	4,264,832	100	316,465	7.42%
Temperate grasslands	8,976,591	495	88,127	0.98%
Mixed mountain systems	10,633,145	2,766	967,130	9.10%
Mixed island systems	3,252,563	1,980	530,676	16.32%
Lake systems	517,695	66	5,814	1.12%
TOTAL	**145,605,658**	**169,636**	**9,489,665**	**6.52%**

To assess representativeness, it is necessary to compile one or more relevant classifications of types. The main requirement is that the typologies be appropriate to the scale of planning, and that they be based on the best available science. It also helps if a typology relates to an established international scheme (e.g. Udvardy 1975). The conclusions will always be sensitive to the classification used, so alternative analyses using different schemes and/or using different numbers of classes within the same general scheme should be tested or synthesised. Even in countries with detailed resource inventories and substantial research capacity, classification schemes are capable of refinement, and in that sense remain provisional. Computer-based methods make it much easier to assess the implications of different classifications; the desirable iterative analyses are usually impractical by any other method.

It is then necessary to identify the areas which might be available as examples of each environment type. While it is simplest to identify for presence-only (regardless of the area of the type contained), it is usually desirable for reasons of adequacy (see below) to undertake the analysis using an appropriate range of threshold criteria – such as 1, 2, 5, or 10% of the total extent of the environment type contained within the candidate area – or as defined by a single threshold level at the outset. In all cases, the threshold level is essentially arbitrary, or at best defined by other criteria such as adequacy and management practicality. The candidate areas then need assessment as to their relative qualities, taking account of the extent of each environment type contained within them, their condition and integrity considerations. Complementarity (the extent to which a candidate area adds to achievement of the representational objective overall) may be more important than high species diversity.

There is an extensive technical literature on this subject. Mackinnon *et al.,* (1986) remains an excellent overview, but should be read in association with more recent contributions (e.g. Margules *et al.,* 1988, 1994, Theberge 1989, Bedward *et al.,* 1992, Belbin 1992, Pressey *et al.,* 1993, *1994,* Scott *et al.,* 1993, Pressey and Logan 1994, Peres and Terborgh 1995, Caughley and Gunn 1996). It may be necessary to combine assessments of reserve coverage which are based on environmental representational objectives (the biogeographic approach) with assessments based on species and habitat conservation objectives (the key species approach). However, a reserve system should not be designed to be representative alone. It should also take account of the need to give protection to refugia areas, rare species habitat, breeding habitat of migratory species and landform features.

3.1.2 Adequacy

> *Integrity, sufficiency of spatial extent and arrangement of contributing units, together with effective management, to support viability of the environmental processes and/or species, populations and communities which make up the biodiversity of the country.*

A wide range of issues must be considered in selecting between alternative designs of national protected area systems. The final location, size and boundaries of contributing areas will be influenced by factors such as (for example, see Figure 1):

- habitat/area requirements of rare or other species and their minimum viable population sizes;

- connectivity between units (corridors) to permit wildlife migration, or occasionally isolation to minimise transfer of disease, predators and the like;

Figure 13-1: Guidelines for the Selection and Design of Protected Areas.

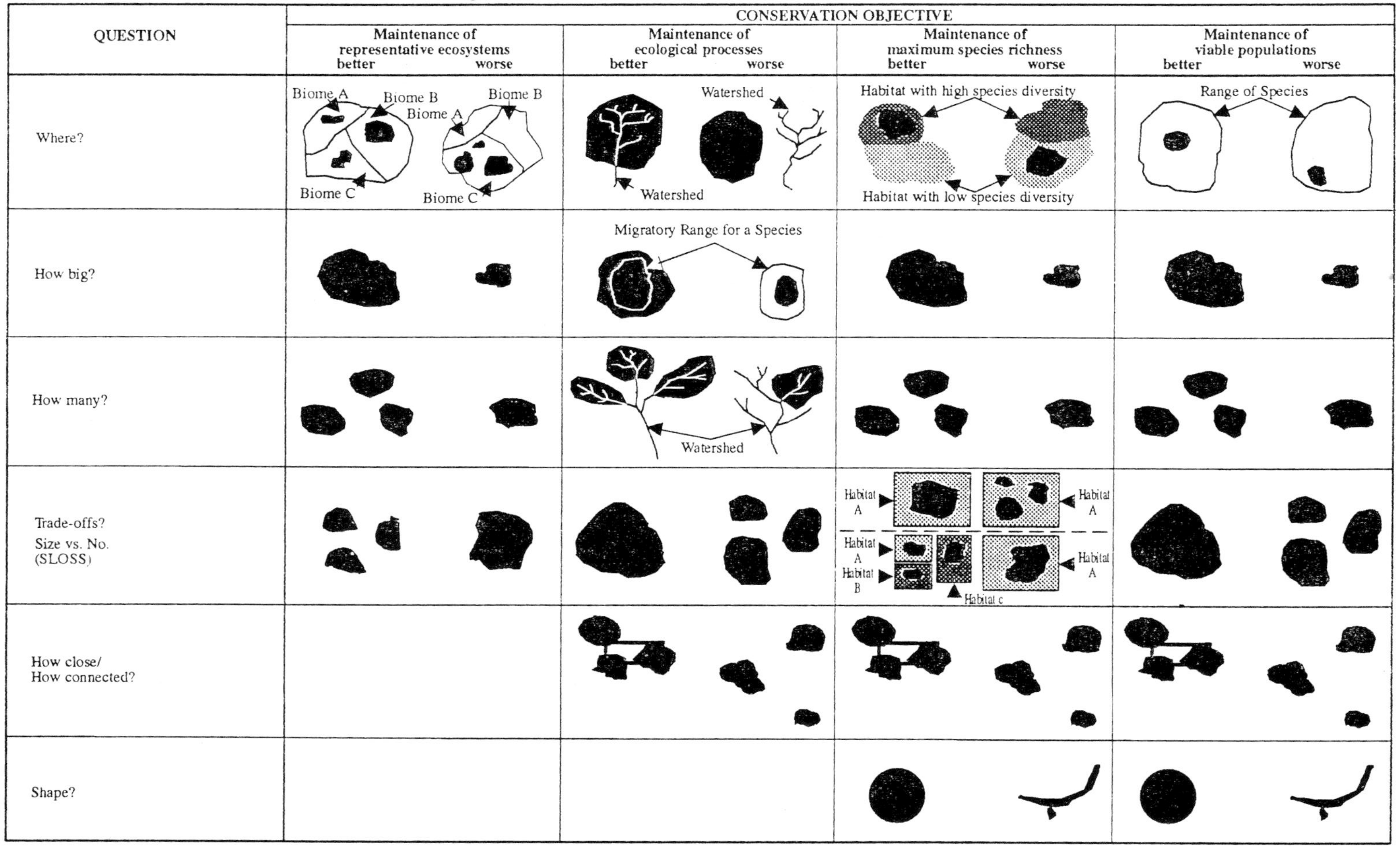

Guidelines for the selection and design of protected areas in relationship to four objectives for conserving living resources. The preferable guideline for the selection and design of protected areas in relationship to the conservation objectives and the question of design is presented under the column labeled "better," whereas the less preferable guideline is presented under the column labeled "worse".
Source: Lusigi, 1992.

- perimeter/area relationships;

- natural system linkages and boundaries – e.g. watersheds (surface and groundwater), volcanism, ocean currents, aeolian or other active geomorphic systems;

- accessibility to undertake management operations or inaccessibility to deter potentially impacting activity;

- existing degradation or external threats;

- traditional use, occupancy and sustainability; and

- cost of achieving protected area status (most commonly land acquisition, compensation or transfer costs, or costs of establishing co-management mechanisms).

3.1.3 Coherence and complementarity

Positive contribution of each site towards the whole.

Each site needs to add value to the national system of protected areas, in quality as well as quantity. There is little point in increasing the extent or number of protected areas unless this brings benefits at least in proportion to the costs.

3.1.4 Consistency

Application of management objectives, policies and classifications under comparable conditions in standard ways, so that the purpose of each unit is clear to all and to maximise the chance that management and use support the objectives.

Consistency focuses on the links between objectives and action. One of the main purposes of the IUCN protected areas management classification is to promote a scheme of protected area types based on management objectives, and emphasising that management should flow consistently from those objectives.

3.1.5 Cost effectiveness, efficiency and equity

Appropriate balance between the costs and benefits, and appropriate equity in their distribution; includes efficiency: the minimum number and area of protected areas needed to achieve system objectives.

The establishment and management of protected areas is a kind of social contract. They are set up and run for the purpose of realising certain benefits for society. People will therefore need to be assured that they are effective, represent value for money, and are managed in a way which is equitable in terms of their impact on communities.

3.2 System components and interactions

3.2.1 Integrating system plans into the international context

The overriding objective of a National System Plan is to increase the effectiveness of *in situ* biodiversity conservation. IUCN has suggested that the long term success of *in situ* conservation requires that the global network of protected areas comprise a representative sample of each of the world's different ecosystems. In order to maximise the efficiency with which this is done, a global view is needed.

For example, if a country no longer has a significant proportion of its old growth forests remaining, it will be necessary to compensate for this shortfall by protecting a relatively larger proportion of such forests in neighbouring countries. So it is important that effective national system planning promotes cooperation between States.

Viewing the National System Plan in an international context may also help identify opportunities to increase conservation efficiency through cooperation. Among other things, the lessons learned from island bio-geography research have taught us that a few large protected areas more effectively conserve biodiversity than a series of small ones. As a result, transboundary protected areas may offer opportunities to increase the effectiveness of protected areas, and at a lower cost.

Therefore, it is necessary that each country's system plan acknowledge the conservation needs of the region, and especially those areas of land and sea that adjoin neighbouring States. Possibilities for cooperative approaches should be identified and joint conservation initiatives should be fostered, especially the creation of transboundary protected areas. Among other benefits, international collaboration:

■ efficiently complements the conservation efforts of both countries;

■ promotes better relations between the states (e.g. "Peace Parks"); and

■ facilitates the sharing of information, experience and training capacity.

Although informal arrangements between States can and occasionally do result in collaboration, experience has shown that it is preferable to pursue formal accords. Such commitments can be facilitated by the existing framework of international cooperation. The Biological Diversity, World Heritage, and Ramsar Conventions, initiatives such as WWF's Global 200 Project, UNESCO's Man and the Biosphere Programme, and organisations such as IUCN's World Commission on Protected Areas provide leadership for international cooperation. Agreements made under the Convention on Migratory Species and the Pan European Biodiversity and Landscape Strategy provide specific examples of how international coordination can be organised and formally endorsed at the regional level.

3.2.2 Bio-regional planning

Within each country the fundamental aim of conservation should be the care of **all** land and water. Thus, while these guidelines relate to protected areas, it is important not to lose sight of the many links to land use planning and sustainable economic and social development at a broader scale. Bio-regional planning provides a means of making those connections (see, for example, Miller 1996). This approach looks beyond the boundaries of strictly protected areas, to include the establishment of buffer and support zones around them, the creation of corridors of ecologically- friendly land use between them and the restoration of areas which have lost their ecological value. In this way, bio-regional planning can help to strengthen protected areas and place them within a national strategy for conservation. Many of the ideas promoted through bio-regional planning have of course been given more concrete forms through biosphere reserves (see, for example, UNESCO 1996 and Batisse 1997).

A national system plan for protected areas should therefore address the needs of protected areas in the broader context offered by bio-regional planning.

3.2.3 IUCN Protected Area Management Categories

The IUCN scheme (chapter 1.3; also Appendix 2) provides a range of available categories of protected areas, each suited to particular needs and each capable of contributing towards regional, national or international goals of biodiversity conservation. Each category offers different potential in managing the interaction between the protected area and its community and environmental context, thereby producing different benefits for the country. Units in a national protected area system falling under one category thus support those in other categories; and each needs to be planned in conjunction with those in other categories.

Most countries have a considerable number of protected areas. Overviews of the range of units, their management classification and status are available at global or

Under the zoning system of Desembarco del Granma National Park, Cuba, there is provision for a Marine Protected Landscape (Category V) in the zone of Cabo Cruz, where traditional and limited commercial fisheries are allowed.

regional levels (IUCN 1992b, 1994b, McNeely *et al.*, 1994), but it is common for there to be limited systematic appraisal at a national level. Under the former (IUCN 1978) classification scheme (compared with IUCN 1994), it was likely that a large number of protected areas in many countries were misclassified (in the sense that the category to which they were assigned did not reflect their primary purpose).

The adoption by IUCN of the 1994 category guidelines called for a fresh look at the most appropriate classification for each unit within the system. It is widely recognised that there is scope for greater application of the more flexible categories (IUCN 1994), especially V (protected landscape/seascape) and VI (managed resource protected area). A national system plan should clearly identify the links between that country's scheme and all six categories of the IUCN classification.

4. The scope of a system plan

System planning needs to begin by addressing the inter-relationships between protected areas, and between protected areas and the wider context. While the specific issues, and their priority, depend largely on the individual characteristics of each country, the planning process should systematically address a number of general questions, as are outlined in Box 8.

The need to assess these and any other relevant questions is thrown into sharp relief by the deterioration of the condition of protected areas in some regions. There is serious and extensive degradation from activities such as hunting, overgrazing, tree cutting and gathering of wild produce. Sometimes there is full-scale commercial logging or mining, or military occupation. In some cases these impacts appear to have completely eliminated the significant resources which were the reason for establishing the protected area in the first place.

Box 8. Questions relating to scope that need to be addressed in preparing a national system plan for protected areas

- What is the state of development of the system and its associated institutions? What are the historical, social, cultural, economic or other factors which explain the present state and what are their implications for further progress?

- What are the links between protected areas and other national planning, including on biodiversity or land use matters? In particular, what are the links with national biodiversity plans, national environmental plans or national plans for ecologically sustainable development?

- What are the trends in impacts (local, regional, national, international) that have implications for sustainability of protected areas? Examples include changes in security, land use, demography, public health or technology.

- What are the current or possible impacts stemming from protected areas on adjacent lands and/or people? Do protected areas harbour (potential or actual) diseases or pests? Do park wildlife populations have adverse interactions with surrounding human settlements or land use?

- Do protected areas provide important resources (e.g. food, forage, fuel) for local peoples? Is this use sustainable currently and in the future? Are there other options for meeting these needs?

■ What are the mechanisms for maintaining effective links between protected areas and sustainable land use management on lands allocated to other uses?

■ Have protected areas potential for providing social or economic benefits and if so at which of the levels – local, regional, national, international? How will equity issues be addressed? If there are significant economic or other benefits, how will they be shared equitably between local peoples and other sectors?

■ Does the present protected area system function as a whole? Is it reasonably complete and representative? Is there sufficient connectivity? Do the different levels of government and other institutions involved with protected areas support each other? and

■ What are the opportunities for (and constraints on) transboundary collaboration?

Such large scale damage of protected areas should be seen in a context of widespread deforestation, desertification, range degradation, depletion of wildlife populations, or other environmental deterioration, over much of the land and marine area of many countries. There have also been important changes in the hydrological regime of major rivers, with many consequent environmental changes, including widespread dieback or removal of important natural habitats. These escalating environmental trends are linked to population growth and aspects of economic development, or to responses to these. In many countries there are also very serious management obstacles posed by recession, war, insurgency, corruption or drug trafficking. As an example, during early 1995 in just four of the countries of Central America, 42 park personnel were killed on duty when their work brought them into contact with illegal drug and mining activities.

Training session on Community Management of Protected Areas as part of the activities of the Regional Community Forestry Training Centre (RECOFTC) in Thailand. Training includes field activities, in this case in Chalerm Rattanakosin National Park.

The following sections examine some particular issues which need special consideration in system planning.

4.1 Information

Good information can improve the quality of decision making. Actions (including the decision to take no action) always have consequences. Good information enhances the ability to predict these consequences. Information is also essential in the identification of priorities and testing trade-offs. Addressing the issue of representativeness, or other system characteristics (see chapter 3.1) requires at least a basic level of information about biodiversity and earth features right across the country, as well as information

---

Box 9. Information and national system plans for protected areas – a checklist

- a range of information is required, such as health, social, demographic, economic and land use data, not just environmental or natural resource management information. The "basics" in terms of information for protected area system planning are:

  - basic natural resource data;

  - basic information on local communities;

  - forward government plans for land use;

  - existing pattern of land use;

- it is important to be open about the biases inherent in information and to specify assumptions;

- added value of information usually occurs when different disciplines work together;

- analysis and interpretation of data should be given as much attention as its collection;

- monitoring needs to be given more emphasis, and linked to evaluation, and the taking of corrective action;

- relevant knowledge depends on stakeholders: information does not only come from computers – qualitative and local knowledge can be very important;

- technology must be applicable to the setting in which it is applied;

- knowledge is always changing: decisions cannot wait for all the data to be collected; and

- information collection and management should be linked to the building of institutional capacity: local staff knowledge can be significant and should not be ignored (institutional memory is valuable).

Traditional practices, such as pastoralism, are allowed under buffer zone management in the Tatra Biosphere Reserve, Poland.

about existing protected areas. Biophysical information needs to be complemented by appropriate social and economic data.

Priority should be given to gathering information on the most important conservation needs and issues, some elements of which are described in Box 9.

4.2 Models, concepts and definitions

The "exclusive" use concept applied to many protected areas, especially "national parks", has created great resentment and resistance among local people and political leaders in some parts of the world. Indeed, because of the exclusive connotations associated with the term "national park" the title has sometimes been effective in ensuring that certain proposed areas have NOT become protected areas. Had a more flexible approach been taken, it is possible that some useful form of protection of the area would have been secured. The wider application of IUCN categories V and VI, as alternative models to category II, has potential here.

A uniform approach is not workable. There needs to be a range of different solutions responding to different environments and to the many different social and cultural contexts. Within federal countries, national system plans should recognise the diversity among the provinces, with a range of approaches appropriate to provincial situations and priorities: this is particularly relevant given the trend to decentralise responsibility for conservation management. Even within unitary government systems, or relatively small countries, the same principles apply in relation to local government areas and municipalities, many of which are managing protected areas.

There is a need also to involve private, tribal and community lands in a country's protected area system. Only a limited percentage of the land area of most countries (in some cases very little) is held directly by the government, so it is not likely to be effective for a protected areas programme to be based exclusively on government land. Extension of protected areas into non-government land should involve partnership with the existing holders of lands of conservation value; indeed the initiative to set up protected areas may come from those non-governmental communities. Many countries are now examining ways in which such partnerships can be developed.

While central government must continue to have an overall leadership function in relation to all protected areas as well as a specific role in management of some of them, it is also clear there is strong support for co-management and for a range of models involving people resident within protected areas (e.g. Amend and Amend 1995, Kemf 1993, West and Brechin 1991; Borrini-Feyerabend, 1997). There are already many examples – not always formally recognised as protected areas but effectively functioning as such – where the main management responsibility has been undertaken by local communities, with the support in various ways of NGOs and governments. However, such co-operation is difficult in the absence of proper procedures to identify and reconcile (or accommodate) prior rights and traditional uses before protected areas are set up.

In some countries, natural resource protection measures sometimes appear inflexible, and do not necessarily promote a sense of responsibility among local communities. But while inflexible legislative arrangements make it difficult to encourage local people to become involved in sustainable management programmes, some protected area categories (e.g. V, VI) do allow for sustainable harvest. This appears to offer the prospect of raising local interest in resource conservation (and reducing illegal activities or harmful habitat disturbance). When most of the revenue stays in the local area, this substantially increases the incentives for species and habitat management on the part of local people and helps address their economic and social needs. However, such a strategy depends on the rate of use being consistent with long term conservation of the species concerned.

The fast growing diversity of approaches to protected areas management, involving government at every level, local communities, indigenous peoples, NGOs, private owners and so forth, is a welcome trend. The role of the national system plan is to provide a framework within which all these actors can identify, and make, their distinctive contribution to the national conservation effort. It is therefore very important that they are involved in the plan-making process itself, a subject addressed in later chapters.

5. Requirements for the successful implementation of a system plan

System planning is not likely to be successful unless implementation is considered just as carefully, and has as much influence on planning thinking, as the issues discussed in the previous section. Again, exercise of considerable judgement is required. Some of the questions which need to be asked are presented in Box 10.

Box 10. Implementation issues to be addressed in preparing a national system plan for protected areas

■ How are the component parts of the national system co-ordinated? How do different players interact and which of them have which interests, powers, responsibilities and capacities? For instance, the appropriate institutional arrangements and other mechanisms for a physically large federal country will be radically different from a compact unitary state.

■ What are the implications for implementation of the structure of the state (e.g. the system of government and the organisation of the economy), and of the geographic and economic realities? What kinds of institutions currently exist?

■ What are the implications of the particular balance in a country between government sovereignty, land use planning controls and co-ordination between the state, regions and local communities, resource ownership (tenure), and economic incentives?

■ What linkages or potential links exist between the protected area institutions in the country and internationally?

■ How do the institutions of the state interact with corporate, private and community institutions and mechanisms, and what are the structural implications for supporting the protected area system?

■ What are the priority needs: new mechanisms, structures, institutions, expertise, training, experience, money, information, better communication, equipment and infrastructure? and

■ What range of options is there for providing for effective implementation?

Protected area planning and management should be linked at the system level with National Conservation Strategies and a National Biodiversity Strategy and Action Plan. Development of a system plan must not be exclusively a "top-down" process;

rather, it must have effective two-way involvement with provincial and/or local governments as well as with appropriate local communities and NGOs. The precise nature and level of involvement must be appropriate to the cultural, political and legal context. Planning should be linked to relevant field demonstration projects, to provide case examples, to give a continuing sense of co-operation and commitment, and to ensure that planning is based in reality.

There is a clear distinction between national **system** planning and **management** planning at the site level. The system plan examines the country as a whole; it provides national-level co-ordination with other planning and between the various different units of a national system; it provides a programme for the several units to achieve the desired characteristics of a coherent system. However, the system plan should also provide guidelines for management planning at the site level. Thus, while management planning for individual system units should not form part of the national system plan *per se*, the system plan should provide a broad framework for management plans. Integration of national, regional and local management policies, reconciliation of local conflicts, articulation of specific objectives, management programmes and zoning controls, and resolution of many other important site-level issues, are necessary tasks which can usually best be undertaken at the site level in management plans for individual system units (see Figure 2).

Particular issues which need to be considered in assessing implementation implications for system planning are discussed in the following sections.

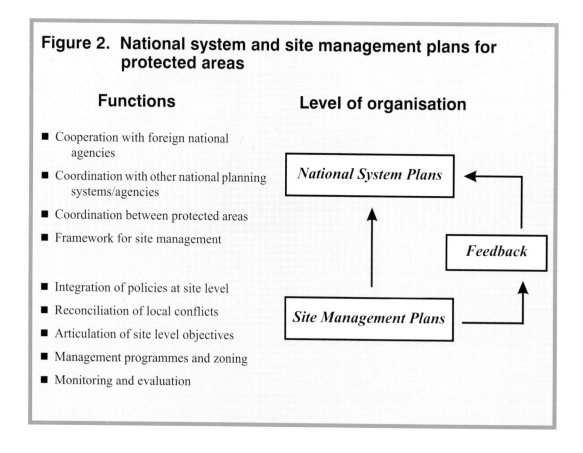

Figure 2. National system and site management plans for protected areas

Functions	Level of organisation
■ Cooperation with foreign national agencies	
■ Coordination with other national planning systems/agencies	*National System Plans*
■ Coordination between protected areas	
■ Framework for site management	*Feedback*
■ Integration of policies at site level	
■ Reconciliation of local conflicts	
■ Articulation of site level objectives	*Site Management Plans*
■ Management programmes and zoning	
■ Monitoring and evaluation	

5.1 Community involvement and consultation

Most protected areas have people living in or adjoining them. The successful establishment and maintenance of protected areas in most societies will depend on a co-operative relationship between local communities and protected area managers. While local communities are in a position to ensure that a protected area will "fail" unless their concerns are met in some appropriate way, they also have knowledge which can be crucial to the successful management of protected areas.

Local communities living in or adjoining protected areas should therefore be considered as a special group in the establishment and management of protected areas. Protected areas cannot be separated from the need for local peoples to meet their aspirations for economic development and a better quality of life. This principle is a clear commitment from the World Parks Congress, embodied in the Caracas Action Plan (McNeely 1993).

Most if not all protected area management issues are ultimately connected with the social and economic needs of people. The problem is exacerbated by rapid population growth and shortfall in services and infrastructure. These factors accelerate environmental degradation and make it more difficult to manage many protected areas.

Local people have a range of interests in protected areas. It is desirable to maximise the coincidence of those interests with protection and management. Where communities directly benefit from protected areas there is a greater likelihood of success of the community involvement programme (see Box 11).

Consultation should extend beyond the local community to include all important stakeholders. As part of the institutional and decision framework within which protected areas are managed, stakeholders – such as tourism operations, water and energy supply companies, and the media – are potentially very influential. Without their co-operation, the effective development of a protected area system may be

Training session on social assessments and discussions with one of the elders of a Karen minority, close to Chalerm Rattanakosin National Park, Thailand

29

Box 11. Local people and protected areas – key principles

- local people should be fully involved in making decisions about management objectives or policies;

- the needs of local communities should be assessed and information arising from these consultations should be used in protected area planning and management;

- the creation and management of protected areas should be co-ordinated with the provision of infrastructure and services, as well as development of sustainable rural land use;

- the maintenance of agricultural biodiversity, fuel supply, livestock bloodlines, forage systems and range management should be assured because local peoples may not have viable options for supporting protected area management until they achieve higher productivity in their core economic activities and meet their basic needs;

- the selection and training of local protected area staff should be recognised as critical in relation to community involvement. Skills in areas such as community consultation need to be developed; and

- there should be evaluation and analysis of successful models of community involvement, with wide dissemination of the results. There also needs to be sharing of experience between those working in different cultural and economic contexts.

---

difficult. Failure to consult with some stakeholders may create obstacles, and pass up opportunities for creative and sustainable solutions to problems.

Development of a national protected area system plan should therefore enable relevant stakeholders (whatever the nature of their interest in the system, in individual units, or in the consequences of policy choices, and whatever their economic, social or political status in the local, national or international context) to be identified and heard at an early stage. However, precise methods, frequency and sequence of consultative interactions should accord to the issues and interests of different stakeholder groups. The consultation strategy must be appropriate to the capacities and interests of the different groups, as well as relevant to the issues associated with the protected area system.

5.2 Financing

The budgets of protected area agencies have fallen sharply in many countries in recent decades. Since limited funds are usually the main constraint on management, the success of the system plan will depend on the development of clear fund-raising and investment strategies. In countries where it is relevant, this may be one way of linking protected area needs with the international donor community.

The system plan itself should identify funding priorities, and encourage funding from prospective sources. It should be based on a pragmatic assessment of the resources which need to be mobilised for its implementation.

Protected area managers need to be more aggressive and effective in arguing the social and economic benefits of investment in protected areas and their management. It may be helpful to form partnerships for this purpose with other stakeholders with an economic and social interest in biodiversity conservation.

5.3 Commitment and political support

Without adequate social, political and financial support, protected area systems will fail. Key target groups are listed in Box 12.

Box 12. Target groups for national system plans for protected areas

■ **local communities**, whose support is essential for protected area viability. The involvement referred to in 5.1 is an important strategy for achieving this;

■ **decision makers and politicians** at all levels whose support is critical and which will be reflected in financial and institutional assistance. The need is to identify those people who will influence decision making and work with them in the development and implementation of a system plan. In building support, benefits of protected areas need to be clearly identified and promoted. For example, WCPA has prepared a draft document about the economic benefits of protected areas (CNPPA 1996) and a final version will be published in this guideline series;

■ **the national and local media**, who can help shape public opinion and raise public awareness;

■ **international funding sources**; and

■ **international conventions** etc. which can be used to link country-level protected area system planning to external opportunities such as those provided under the Convention on Biological Diversity, and the World Heritage and Ramsar Conventions.

The system plan should be drawn up in consultation with this range of interest-groups in mind and if necessary its publication should be supported by other materials (e.g. summary documents in user-friendly language or videos) designed to secure their support for the plan's aims.

5.4 Institutions

Discussion of institutions does not refer only to national government protected area agencies, but includes:

■ different levels of government;

■ agencies exercising a wide range of functions in the government and NGO sectors; and

■ mechanisms for linking between these, and with the private sector.

System plans must be capable of being implemented within the resources available to institutions. Unless there are effective institutions there will be no effective protected areas. However, countries are at very different levels in relation to their capacities to provide resources to the institutions which manage protected areas.

In the context of preparing for the national system plan, the following points need careful consideration:

■ in most countries there is a need to improve co-ordination between government departments, with parastatals and other agencies, among different levels of government, and between the government and NGO sector, so as to maximise the effectiveness of the institutions engaged in protected areas work;

■ cross-border liaison is often needed to integrate opportunities for conservation management in neighbouring countries – examples include seasonal migrations of herbivores across natural borders – and to implement programmes of complementary action; such cross-border co-operation may require innovative mechanisms and institutions (see also 3.2.1);

■ an effective protected area institution is one which satisfies the requirements in Box 13;

■ effective protected area management requires stable institutions: since the institutional environment must encourage the right staff to stay in the right jobs, there is a need for long term continuity, both in institutional and staff terms;

■ strong and effective leadership is crucial within a protected area agency;

■ while it is preferable to work through established institutions, it should also be recognised that sometimes there are dysfunctional institutions which are an obstacle to progress;

■ it is essential to focus on mechanisms for achieving objectives, not just arguing for new or changed organisations: more complex institutional arrangements are not necessarily better;

■ it is important to develop a sense of ownership among different institutions towards the *whole* protected areas system and not only specific areas; and

■ it is desirable to cultivate an institutional memory in protected area institutions, based upon learning from experience, sharing experience, valuing the role of others, and making efficient use of (but not relying on) outside consultancy expertise.

Box 13. Effective protected area institutions – a check list

◾ are responsive to the needs of its stakeholders;

◾ can attract and retain the right staff;

◾ are able to develop a positive attitude and commitment of the staff at all levels;

◾ ideally, have a strongly decentralised structure, where field level staff have a say in decisions which effect their activities;

◾ have a strong sense of identity, particularly at the field level, so that the field level staff feel part of the whole;

◾ have institutional transparency and effective information flow between and within all levels of the institution;

◾ have a stable and long term funding base (reliance on government subventions for viability of an organisation may be less suitable than parastatal arrangements where there is greater ability to raise and retain revenue);

◾ have an appropriate balance between centralised and decentralised decisions; and

◾ have a good system of evaluation and monitoring.

Community-based protected area management training session in Chalerm Rattanakosin National Park, Thailand.

5.5 Training

Protected area management training is a priority. However, the need is broader than the traditional focus on resource use aspects, so as to give more emphasis to techniques of community involvement, expertise in negotiating and resolving disputes, and the development of managerial and information technology skills. Recent trends towards such a broader approach need support, as does the targeting of training to priority needs.

Particularly in developing countries, there is a need to build applied research capacity in universities, especially in integrative and multidisciplinary approaches to environmental management. It is desirable to get university and agency personnel working together so that managers better understand the capacities, and constraints, of research processes; and so that researchers better understand management priorities and constraints. Other IUCN guidelines (Harmon 1994) provide advice on this issue.

Appropriate skills and reward structures need to be developed (e.g. in relation to local community involvement skills). In most countries there is a need to build the practical experience of people at local and provincial levels, so that there is a much greater pool of well trained, talented and experienced people to implement participatory field projects.

In this context, the role of the national system plan is to identify the training needs for the country and to put forward a strategy for meeting those, using national and regional institutions, with international assistance when appropriate.

5.6 Partnerships

There is a world-wide trend in devolution of natural resource management away from central government towards provincial and local government, community based groups and indigenous peoples, NGOs, the corporate sector and private individuals. This trend calls for mutually beneficial partnerships to be developed if protected areas are to succeed.

In considering the role of partnerships within the national system plan, these points should be noted:

- Partners may be found in unexpected places (e.g, local communities, the military, the private sector). The need is to open dialogue and to look for areas of mutual benefit. Partnerships will only work when:

  - there is mutual interest;

  - there is mutual benefit;

  - the partners have something to contribute;

- Effective partnership will broaden ownership and commitment, and therefore increase the effectiveness and sustainability of implementation. Partnerships must lead to something; they are not a means in themselves. Realistic expectations need to be established in relation to what a partnership can achieve; and

■ Partnerships will become increasingly relevant to protected areas as alternative management structures become more common.

NGOs can often be a valuable partner, sitting between – or "buffering" – communities and government. They also help mobilise and target resources and have a unique capacity to mediate between groups who may not otherwise work together. Involvement of NGOs should as far as possible be seen as a bridging process, developing the capacities of local communities to conduct their own affairs and to interact more effectively with government and donor agencies.

6. Outline of a model system plan

A system plan should be appropriate to its context. There is no one best process, structure or scope. It should be the product of the environment, state of development and institutional capacity of the country at the time of its preparation. Plans must change with time. It follows that the form of a plan which is appropriate also depends on where a country has progressed in evolution of its protected area system at the time a particular plan is compiled.

Nonetheless, Box 14 lists some crucial elements which should be included in any national system plan for protected areas.

Box 14. Essential elements of a national system plan for protected areas

- clear statement of objectives, rationale, categories, definitions and future directions for protected areas in the country;

- assessment of conservation status, condition and management viability of the various units ;

- review of how well the system samples the biodiversity and other natural and associated cultural heritage of the country;

- procedures for selecting and designing additional protected areas so that the system as a whole has better characteristics;

- identification of the ways in which activities undertaken at national, regional and local levels interact to fulfil national and regional objectives for a system of protected areas;

- a clear basis for integration and co-ordination of protected areas with other aspects of national planning (e.g. with national biodiversity strategies and so forth, but also with land use, economic and social planning);

- assessment of the existing institutional framework for protected areas (relationships, linkages and responsibilities) and identification of priorities for capacity building;

- priorities for further evolution of the protected area system;

- procedures for deciding the management category most appropriate to each existing and proposed unit, to make best use of the full range of available protected area categories, and to promote identification of the ways in which the different system categories support each other;

- identification of investment needs and priorities for protected areas;

- identification of training and human resource development needs for protected area management; and

- guidelines for preparation and implementation of management policies and site-level management plans.

7. Outline of a process for developing a system plan

If it is to be effective, the plan which is eventually developed for any country must reflect on-ground needs and priorities, and must be "owned" by those who will have to implement it. Therefore adoption of a plan should be mainly the task of the people responsible for protected area matters, although many other stakeholders will need to contribute to its initiation, development and implementation. It will be most effective if it evolves out of a constructive partnership between people, according to the structure of government in the country concerned, at district, provincial and national levels, together with interested NGOs and other stakeholders. It is desirable to include the participation of the local people who live in and around the parks (or have other traditional or economic links with them) in developing the plan. It will necessarily take time for the process to reach a stage where a set of integrated programmes will be identifiable as "the system plan". Issues which should be considered in devising a process which is appropriate to local needs and realities include:

- there is no one "right" process that can be used in every case;

- inputs are required from staff at all levels in a protected area agency, including field staff;

- the process should build up local capacity; and

- there is a need for care with the use of external consultants, because much of the learning and institutional memory goes away with them.

It is suggested that the first stage plan for most countries will consist mainly of a work schedule of the different tasks which need to be undertaken (see also Chapters 4 and 5). Box 15 suggests some key elements that should be scheduled.

Box 15. Suggested work schedule for a national system plan for protected areas

- drafting a statement of the national level rationale for a protected area system;

- statement of the objectives and performance indicators at national level of a protected area system;

- drafting an agreed protocol for a community participatory approach to protected area planning and management;

- appraisal in broad terms of the current condition of each of the existing units of the national protected area system;

- assessment of the distribution of areas of biodiversity and environmental types within the country; assessment of the extent to which the present system covers this; consideration of the implications of designing the optimal reserves plan;

- review of the available legal and informal mechanisms to recognise protected areas and provide for their management, to ensure they permit full advantage to be taken of the flexibility and innovation possible under the revised IUCN management categories; in some cases this may include revision of the "names" for different types of protected area and/or the types of management structures used for particular protected areas;

- evaluation of the most appropriate means of conserving representative examples of biodiversity, and of protecting key natural heritage and associated cultural heritage resources, including whether a protected area is the most appropriate mechanism; and

- systematic review of the most appropriate management category for existing and prospective protected areas; this process requires consideration of the affected local communities and, as appropriate, consultation with local, provincial or state governments.

In most countries there is a need for mechanisms to improve co-ordination between line departments, parastatals and agencies, different levels of government, and different sectors. Working parties should be formed to examine ways of bringing people together, such as:

- developing better communications between all major groups of government (including, in federal countries, at provincial as well as local and national levels) on protected area and related matters;

- establishing field seminars or workshops where people from a range of work situations around the country see for themselves the models which work and understand the factors behind successful and not so successful field examples;

- providing a forum (e.g. newsletter, electronic notice board) for regular exchange of ideas between different line agencies, levels of government and sectors.

Some of this activity may be most appropriately handled by central government. Other tasks might be more readily handled by sub committees or working groups. Some new approaches may be needed to bridge government and NGO sectors.

8. Implementation

Plans are only as good as the action they lead to. Too many plans are long on content and short on delivery. If national system plans for protected areas are to avoid this fate, then the following are essential:

- in their preparation, a realistic appraisal should be made of what can be achieved within the resources likely to be available so that the recommendations are recognised as being "in the real world" (e.g. avoid "blue sky" plan-making);

- the plan itself should identify the resource implications of its proposals and the action needed to secure these (e.g. funds to be sought from international donors);

- the plan should be prepared through a process which involves building the support needed from government, local communities and other stakeholders (e.g. through a "round-table" process convened by government);

- the plan should clearly identify who is to do what, and encourage the institutions for implementation to become more sustainable and improve their prospects for self-sufficiency;

- there should be direct links between the system plan as a national tool and the local action required to give effect to these (e.g. a clear connection between the system plan and the site-based management plans);

- the plan itself should be clearly presented, attractive and easy to read: it may need to be accompanied by supporting materials (e.g. summaries for different audiences or videos) and a strategy for its promotion (e.g. through a series of local public meetings); and

- there should be arrangements for monitoring and evaluation so that priorities can be adjusted in the light of experience.

9. Monitoring and evaluation

Differences between theory and reality, between intention and management performance, and between data and knowledge, have been highlighted at several points in this guideline. The national system plan should put in place the monitoring and evaluation arrangements required to ensure that there is a close fit between plan and reality, and in particular these arrangements should:

- establish the response to the plan (e.g. the take up of recommendations);

- establish, as far as possible, the effects upon the purposes for which protected areas have been established (e.g. on wildlife population trends);

- in light of the above, identify any remedial action required, or any adjustments in the content of the plan itself; and

- if necessary, trigger a review of the plan itself.

The monitoring arrangements which are required will need to include those at the level of individual protected areas, so as to facilitate the gathering and evaluation of appropriate data which will permit evaluation of performance of the system as a whole. In this way, the plan will develop the capacity – too often missing in the past – to demonstrate whether long-established protected areas have achieved their purposes.

Incorporation of effective mechanisms for promoting and co-ordinating research, monitoring and evaluation are therefore important in:

- building and maintaining support for protected areas;

- devising and refining effective management strategies and practices;

- identifying and/or reforming institutions to enhance management performance;

- making trade-offs between optimal arrangements for protected areas and the needs and interests of other stakeholders who may have or claim an interest in the same areas; and

- making informed choices among strategic options for disposition or management of the network of protected areas.

As mentioned earlier, research and monitoring in protected areas are the subject of separate IUCN guidelines (Harmon 1994).

Appendices

Appendix 1

Convention on Biological Diversity, article 8, "*In situ* conservation"

Note: a fully annotated guide to the convention is provided by Glowka *et al.*, (1994). The Convention was opened for signature at the 1992 UN Conference on Environment and Development in Rio de Janeiro (also known as the "Earth Summit"). The Convention entered into force in December 1993.

"Article 8. *In situ* conservation – Each Contracting Party shall, as far as possible and as appropriate:

(a) Establish a system of protected areas or areas where special measures need to be taken to conserve biological diversity;

(b) Develop, where necessary, guidelines for the selection, establishment and management of protected areas or areas where special measures need to be taken to conserve biological diversity;

(c) Regulate or manage biological resources important for the conservation of biological diversity whether within or outside protected areas, with a view to ensuring their conservation and sustainable use;

(d) Promote the protection of ecosystems, natural habitats and the maintenance of viable populations of species in natural surroundings;

(e) Promote environmentally sound and sustainable development in areas adjacent to protected areas with a view to further protection of these areas;

(f) Rehabilitate and restore degraded ecosystems and promote the recovery of threatened species, *inter alia*, through the development and implementation of plans or other management strategies;

(g) Establish or maintain means to regulate, manage or control the risks associated with the use and release of living modified organisms resulting from biotechnology which are likely to have adverse environmental impacts that could affect the conservation and sustainable use of biological diversity, taking also into account the risks to human health;

(h) Prevent the introduction of, control or eradicate those alien species which threaten ecosystems, habitats or species;

(i) Endeavour to provide the conditions needed for compatibility between present uses and the conservation of biological diversity and the sustainable use of its components;

(j) Subject to its national legislation, respect, preserve and maintain knowledge, innovations and practices of indigenous and local communities embodying traditional lifestyles relevant for the conservation and sustainable use of biological diversity and promote their wider application with the approval and involvement of the holders of such knowledge, innovations and practices and encourage the equitable sharing of the benefits arising from the utilisation of such knowledge, innovations and practices;

(k) Develop or maintain necessary legislation and/or other regulatory provisions for the protection of threatened species and populations;

(l) Where a significant adverse effect on biological diversity has been determined pursuant to Article 7, regulate or manage the relevant processes and categories of activities; and

(m) Co-operate in providing financial and other support for *in situ* conservation outlined in subparagraphs (a) to (l) above, particularly to developing countries."

Appendix 2

Protected area categories and management objectives

The current IUCN WCPA categories (IUCN 1994a) are as follows:

I.   Strict protection

       a.   Strict Nature Reserve

       b.   Wilderness Area

II.   Ecosystem conservation and recreation (National Park)

III.   Conservation of natural features (Natural Monument)

IV.   Conservation through active management (Habitat/Species Management Area)

V.   Landscape/seascape conservation and recreation (Protected Landscape/seascape)

VI.   Sustainable use of natural ecosystems (Managed Resource Protected Area)

The mix of management objectives relevant to each of the categories is summarised in the following table (IUCN 1994, p.8):

Management objective	Ia	Ib	II	III	IV	V	VI
Scientific research	1	3	2	2	2	2	3
Wilderness protection	2	1	2	3	3	–	2
Preservation of species and genetic diversity	1	2	1	1	1	2	1
Maintenance of environmental services	2	1	1	–	1	2	1
Protection of specific natural/cultural features	–	–	2	1	3	1	3
Tourism and recreation	–	2	1	1	3	1	3
Education	–	–	2	2	2	2	3
Sustainable use of resources from natural ecosystems	–	3	3	–	2	2	1
Maintenance of cultural/traditional attributes	–	–	–	–	–	1	2

Key

   1 Primary objective; 2 Secondary objective; 3 Potentially applicable objective; – Not applicable

The definitions, objectives and selection criteria for the categories and sub-categories are summarised as follows (IUCN 1994, part II and p.9):

Category I –   Strict Nature Reserve/Wilderness Area: protected area managed mainly for science or wilderness protection

Category Ia – Strict Nature Reserve: protected area managed mainly for science

Definition: Area of land and/or sea possessing some outstanding or representative ecosystems, geological or physiological features and/or species, available primarily for scientific research and/or environmental monitoring.

Objectives of management:

- to preserve habitats, ecosystems and species in as undisturbed a state as possible

- to maintain genetic resources in a dynamic and evolutionary state

- to maintain established ecological processes

- to safeguard structural landscape features or rock exposures

- to secure examples of the natural environment for scientific studies, environmental monitoring and education, including baseline areas from which all avoidable access is excluded

- to minimise disturbance by careful planning and execution of research and other approved activities

- to limit public access

Guidance for selection:

- The area should be large enough to ensure the integrity of its ecosystems and to accomplish the management objectives for which it is protected.

- The area should be significantly free of direct human intervention and capable of remaining so.

- The conservation of the area's biodiversity should be achievable through protection and not require substantial active management or habitat manipulation (c.f. Category IV).

Equivalent category in IUCN (1978): Scientific Reserve/Strict Nature Reserve.

Category Ib – Wilderness Area: protected area managed mainly for wilderness protection

Definition: Large area of unmodified or slightly modified land, and/or sea, retaining its natural character and influence, without permanent or significant habitation, which is protected and managed so as to preserve its natural condition.

Objectives of management:

- to ensure that future generations have the opportunity to experience understanding and enjoyment of areas that have been largely undisturbed by human action over a long period of time

- to maintain the essential natural attributes and qualities of the environment over the long term

- to provide for public access at levels and of a type which will serve best the physical and spiritual well-being of visitors and maintain the wilderness qualities of the area for present and future generations

- to enable indigenous human communities living at low density and in balance with the available resources to maintain their lifestyle

Guidance for selection:

- The area should possess high natural quality, be governed primarily by the forces of nature, with human disturbance substantially absent, and be likely to continue to display those attributes if managed as proposed.

- The area should contain significant ecological, geological, physiogeographic, or other features of scientific, educational, scenic or historic value.

- The area should offer outstanding opportunities for solitude, enjoyed once the area has been reached, by simple, quiet, non-polluting and non-intrusive means of travel (i.e. non-motorised).

- The area should be of sufficient size to make practical such preservation and use.

Equivalent category in IUCN (1978): no direct equivalent.

Category II – National Park: protected area managed mainly for ecosystem protection and tourism

Definition: Natural area of land and/or sea, designated to (a) protect the ecological integrity of one or more ecosystems for present and future generations, (b) exclude exploitation or occupation inimical to the purposes of designation of the area, and (c) provide a foundation for spiritual, scientific, educational, recreational and visitor opportunities, all of which must be environmentally and culturally compatible.

Objectives of management:

- to protect natural and scenic areas of national and international significance for spiritual, scientific, educational, recreational or tourist purposes

- to perpetuate, in as natural a state as possible, representative examples of physiographic regions, biotic communities, genetic resources, and species, to provide ecological stability and diversity

- to manage visitor use for inspirational, educational, cultural and recreational purposes at a level which will maintain the area in a natural or near natural state

- to eliminate and thereafter prevent exploitation or occupation inimical to the purposes of designation

- to maintain respect for the ecological, geomorphologic, sacred or aesthetic attributes which warranted designation

- to take into account the needs of indigenous people, including subsistence resource use, in so far as these will not adversely affect the other objectives of management

Guidance for selection:

- The area should contain a representative sample of major natural regions, features or scenery, where plant and animal species, habitats and geomorphological sites are of special spiritual, scientific, educational, recreational and tourist significance.

- The area should be large enough to contain one or more entire ecosystems not materially altered by current human occupation or exploitation.

Equivalent category in IUCN 1978: National Park

Category III – Natural Monument: protected area managed mainly for conservation of specific natural features

Definition: Area containing one, or more, specific natural or natural/cultural feature which is of outstanding or unique value because of its inherent rarity, representative or aesthetic qualities or cultural significance.

Objectives of management:

- to protect or preserve in perpetuity specific outstanding natural features because of their natural significance, unique or representational quality, and/or spiritual connotations

- to an extent consistent with the foregoing objective, to provide opportunities for research, education, interpretation and public appreciation

- to eliminate and thereafter prevent exploitation or occupation inimical to the purpose of designation

- to deliver to any resident population such benefits as are consistent with the other objectives of management

Guidance for selection:

- The area should contain one or more features of outstanding significance (appropriate natural features include spectacular waterfalls, caves, craters, fossil beds, sand dunes and marine features, along with unique or representative fauna and flora; associated cultural features might include cave dwellings, cliff-top forts, archaeological sites, or natural sites which have heritage significance to indigenous peoples).

- The area should be large enough to protect the integrity of the feature and its immediately related surroundings.

Equivalent category in IUCN (1978): Natural Monument/Natural Landmark

Category IV – Habitat/Species Management Area: protected area managed mainly for conservation through management intervention

Definition: Area of land and/or sea subject to active intervention for management purposes so as to ensure the maintenance of habitats and/or to meet the requirements of specific species.

Objectives of management:

- to secure and maintain the habitat conditions necessary to protect significant species, groups of species, biotic communities or physical features of the environment where these require specific human manipulation for optimum management

- to facilitate scientific research and environmental monitoring as primary activities associated with sustainable resource management

- to develop limited areas for public education and appreciation of the characteristics of the habitats concerned and of the work of wildlife management

- to eliminate and thereafter prevent exploitation or occupation inimical to the purpose of designation

- to deliver such benefits to people living within the designated area as are consistent with the other objectives of management

Guidance for selection:

- The area should play an important role in the protection of nature and the survival of species (incorporating, as appropriate, breeding areas, wetlands, coral reefs, estuaries, grasslands, forests or spawning areas, including marine feeding beds).

- The area should be one where the protection of the habitat is essential to the well-being of nationally or locally-important flora, or to resident or migratory fauna.

- Conservation of these habitats and species should depend upon active intervention by the management authority, if necessary through habitat manipulation (c.f. Category Ia).

- The size of the area should depend on the habitat requirements of the species to be protected and may range from relatively small to very extensive.

Equivalent category in IUCN (1978): Nature Conservation Reserve/Managed Nature Reserve/Wildlife Sanctuary.

Category V – Protected Landscape/Seascape: protected area managed mainly for landscape/seascape conservation and recreation

Definition: Area of land, with coast and sea as appropriate, where the interaction of people and nature over time has produced an area of distinctive character with significant aesthetic, ecological and/or cultural value, and often with high biological diversity. Safeguarding the integrity of this traditional interaction is vital to the protection, maintenance and evolution of such an area.

Objectives of management:

- to maintain the harmonious interaction of nature and culture through the protection of landscape and/or seascape and the continuation of traditional land uses, building practices and social and cultural manifestations

- to support lifestyles and economic activities which are in harmony with nature and the preservation of the social and cultural fabric of the communities concerned

- to maintain the diversity of landscape and habitat, and of associated species and ecosystems

- to eliminate where necessary, and thereafter prevent, land uses and activities which are inappropriate in scale and/or character

- to provide opportunities for public enjoyment through recreation and tourism appropriate in type and scale to the essential qualities of the areas

- to encourage scientific and educational activities which will contribute to the long term well-being of resident populations and to the development of public support for the environmental protection of such areas

- to bring benefits to, and to contribute to the welfare of, the local community through the provision of natural products (such as forest and fisheries products) and services (such as clean water or income derived from sustainable forms of tourism)

Guidance for selection:

- The area should possess a landscape and/or coastal and island seascape of high scenic quality, with diverse associated habitats, flora and fauna along with manifestations of unique or traditional land-use patterns and social organisations as evidenced in human settlements and local customs, livelihoods, and beliefs.

- The area should provide opportunities for public enjoyment through recreation and tourism within its normal lifestyle and economic activities.

Equivalent category in IUCN (1978): Protected Landscape.

Category VI – Managed Resource Protected Area: protected area managed mainly for the sustainable use of natural ecosystems

Definition: Area containing predominantly unmodified natural systems, managed to ensure long term protection and maintenance of biological diversity, while providing at the same time a sustainable flow of natural products and services to meet community needs. The area must also fit the overall definition of a protected area.

Objectives of management:

- to protect and maintain the biological diversity and other natural values of the area in the long term

- to promote sound management practices for sustainable production purposes

- to protect the natural resource base from being alienated for other land use purposes that would be detrimental to the area's biological diversity

- to contribute to regional and national development

Guidance for selection:

- At least two-thirds of the area should be in, and is planned to remain in, a natural condition, although it may also contain limited areas of modified ecosystems; large commercial plantations are not to be included.

- The area should be large enough to absorb sustainable resource uses without detriment to its overall long-term natural values.

- A management authority must be in place.

Equivalent category in IUCN (1978): no direct equivalent.

Appendix 3

Case examples

3.1 Canada

Canada's national parks system at federal level includes 36 national parks and park reserves, encompassing about 200,000 square kilometres or just over 2% of the country. There are also very substantial additional areas in provincial parks and other reserve categories, as shown in the table. The federal national park system is still considered far from complete and efforts are underway to expand it.

Summary of all protected areas in Canada (at both federal and provincial/territory level; data from IUCN 1994b; note that the classification here is based on IUCN 1978 rather than IUCN 1994, although this would probably not make a substantial difference here)			
Category	Number	Area (km^2)	% national area
I	100	14,811	0.2
II	251	329,404	3.3
III	2	27	–
IV	176	386,766	3.9
V	111	94,446	1
Total	640	825,455	8.3

The designation "national park" is used at federal level only, and planning for establishing new national parks is carried out at the national level. A national park system plan was devised in the early 1970s – a plan that remains essentially unchanged today (Canada, Environment Canada 1991). The system plan is based on the fundamental principle of protecting an outstanding representative example of each of Canada's landscapes. The system plan divides Canada into 39 distinct "national park natural regions" based on physiography and vegetation, such that by representing each region in the national park system, a cross-section of the country will be protected.

Unlike many plans, this one has not been "put on the shelf", but is regularly referenced and has guided federal national park establishment efforts over two decades. This is at least in part because the plan is easily understood by the public and politicians, and because it has worked well in focusing attention on sites that are truly of national significance, thereby helping to fend off the many local proposals submitted by interest groups.

The national parks system plan, last printed in 1991 (Canada, Environment Canada 1991) and currently being updated, paints a picture of each of Canada's 39 national park natural regions. This is accomplished through text, photos and maps. The plan also outlines a five step process generally followed in establishing new national parks, then goes on to review the status of representation and planning studies for each of the thirty nine natural regions. The document is printed in four colours and is 110 pages long. The bulk of it relates to descriptions of the regions. The planning rationale outlined in the "Introduction" (Canada, Environment Canada 1991, pp. 1–9) contains the following structure:

- Canada's natural heritage

- Our national parks

- It started at Banff ...

- A system plan for national parks

- How do new national parks come into being?
  - Identifying representative natural areas
  - Selecting potential park areas
  - Assessing park feasibility
  - Negotiating a new park agreement
  - Establishing a new national park in legislation

- New national parks and Aboriginal people

- Completing the system

For each of the national park natural regions, there is an illustrated description of the land, vegetation, wildlife, status of national parks and progress in identifying and implementing the system plan for that region. The overall status of national park system planning efforts is summarised in one map for ease of reference and understanding.

It is recognised in the plan that identifying, selecting and establishing new national parks can be a long and complex process. The initial part of the process relies on science to identify areas that have a good representation of the wildlife, vegetation, geology and landforms that characterise a natural region. Later steps in the process increasingly require the consideration of factors that are difficult to measure objectively, such as competing land and resource uses, and impacts on the social and economic life of affected communities.

To date, 22 of Canada's 39 national park natural regions have at least one national park, and proposed national park lands are set aside and withdrawn from competing extractive uses in four other regions pending finalisation of park establishment studies and negotiations.

Separate system plans have also been prepared for other sectors and/or by other agencies and levels of government in Canada, setting out future directions for complementary protected areas systems such as provincial parks (e.g. Canada. Province of British Columbia 1993) and national marine conservation areas (e.g. Canada, Department of Canadian Heritage 1995).

Perceived advantages of Canada's national park system plan are:

- It provides a defensible, science-based framework for park establishment (as opposed to an *ad hoc* reactionary approach).

- The plan defines a finite system; this has facilitated gaining the support of other levels of government and the Department of Finance for the system completion objective.

- The plan focuses park establishment activity on priority areas to complete representation of the natural regions (rather than duplicating existing representation) and helps maximise efficiency in deployment of financial and staff resources.

- It is quickly understandable; this translates into both political support and more meaningful stakeholder involvement in the park establishment process.

Factors which should be considered in assessing the transferability of the Canadian approach to other contexts include:

- It is a plan for federal national parks only – rather than a national system plan for all protected areas – in that it relates just to WCPA category II protected areas under federal jurisdiction and has quite limited linkage to reserves in other categories and/or under provincial or other jurisdiction. In this sense, there may still be room for a Canadian national system plan for protected areas which links the national park system plan with plans for other protected area categories and jurisdictions, and which links all protected areas with their wider context.

- The negotiation of federal jurisdiction over proposed national parks reflects the particular realities of the balance in constitutional powers, land ownership and management control under the Canadian federation. It may also reflect a degree of co-operation between federal and provincial levels which will not be as easy to achieve elsewhere. Other federal countries may have quite different balances in the powers, responsibilities, capacities and priorities of different levels of government, despite superficial similarities of structure. While non-federal countries obviously do not need to conduct the same kinds of transactions between government levels, they may in practice still need as much negotiation with stakeholders as characterises the Canadian approach.

- There appears to be a wide consensus in the Canadian case that the initial classification into "national park natural regions", while based on scientific analysis, rests on an essentially arbitrary or subjective choice of defining criteria. Thus, the number and/or boundaries of the natural regions could be quite different if different aspects of the environment were given greater emphasis in defining the differences between regions. If the formulation of regions is different, it is of course likely that the specific examples which will be chosen as representative areas may differ in location and/or boundaries. Science is always developing new insights, so any classification is always open for review. The Canadians put a great deal of effort into achieving consensus and scientific credibility in their classification when the plan was first developed in the 1970s. This effort has been repaid in reasonable stability and acceptability of the classification, although minor boundary adjustments have been incorporated over the years. At another place or another time it will not necessarily be as stable, even if based on the best available science at the time it is developed, for reasons of subsequent scientific advance or social, economic or technological change, or both. Any country faced with this question has to trade off uncertainties stemming from gaps in scientific understanding, or sheer lack of inventory data, against the advantages of having at least a basic plan adopted and in use as a working framework for conservation management.

- One of the factors which helped acceptance and perceived usefulness of the Canadian plan is its simplicity, and the fact that – even though Canada is a relatively rich country – system planners began with a plan which focused on a simple typology (the 39 classes in such a large country inevitably contain considerable internal diversity) and on just one of the categories of protected areas (i.e. II). Other countries may well find practical advantages in beginning with a "cut-down" national system plan, but all must recognise that the broader system does need to be addressed by some means sooner or later.

For further information about Parks Canada system planning, contact:

Murray McComb, Chief, Planning Studies, Park Establishment Branch, Canadian National Parks, 25 Eddy Street, Hull, Quebec, K1A 0M5, Canada. Phone 001 (819) 994 2300, fax 001 (819) 994 5140, internet: murray_mccomb@pch.gc.ca

3.2 Lao PDR

The Lao PDR is a compact, landlocked, unitary country. Work on a national network of protected areas only began in the late 1980s (Salter and Phanthavong 1989). The country retains a relatively high extent of forest cover for South-east Asia, although much of it is disturbed. As well as regionally significant evergreen forests, the country contains habitat for a number of endangered or threatened species (Berkmüller and others 1995, Chape 1996).

The twenty areas which have been formally declared as National Biological Conservation Areas [NBCAs] to date comprise almost 12.5% (~30,000 km^2) of the country (Chape 1996). Their management concept is most readily compared with WCPA category VI (managed resource protected area – *Appendix 2*), in that in practice they are at present subject to occupation and resource use. The intention, however, is to achieve a range of the more conservative IUCN categories (*Appendix 2*), in at least core areas (Berkmüller and others 1995, Chape 1996). As well as the NBCAs, there are also various other categories of land under provincial management, some of which may be considered as protected areas, and other nationally managed lands which contribute to biodiversity conservation.

The model used in the Lao PDR case is based on participatory management, with a phased shift of management emphasis within the protected area boundaries. Of the identified NBCAs, only seven have yet been established in management terms. Even in those cases, management involves a phased transition, with negotiated boundaries and shift to greater sustainability, and progressive withdrawal of agreed core areas from exploitation.

The system plan gives substantial emphasis to institution-building and implementation. It is recognised that the plan is a vehicle for allocating foreign aid into priority areas, and that the rate of implementation will be influenced by the flow of aid.

The structure of the system plan and status report is as follows (Berkmüller and others 1995):

Protected area system planning

- Scope of the report
- Method
- Overview of progress since mid-1993
- Coverage by biogeographic sub-unit
- Coverage by forest type
    - Constraints and criteria
    - Current forest type coverage
- Altitude coverage
- Setting priorities
    - Contribution to good quality forest cover
    - Habitat ranking of individual NBCAs
- System planning in the coming years
    - Provincial protected areas
    - Corridors and transboundary reserves

Management and policy considerations

- Designations

- Management implementation schedule
- Management objectives and approach
  - Objectives
  - Management phases
- Years 1 to 3 of management
  - Evaluations of past management experience
  - Adjustments to the management model
  - Protected area focused activities
  - Village focused activities
- Other management concerns
  - Boundaries and buffer zones
  - Protection and regulations
  - Socio-economic and land use surveys
  - Wildlife and botanical surveys
  - The shifting cultivation problem
  - Monitoring
  - Budget
- Policy issues
  - Policy implementation
  - Donor agency co-ordination
  - Role of province and districts
  - Hydropower development and road construction

Institutional considerations and human resources

- Internal organisation
- Staff requirements (field)
- Staff requirements (headquarters)
- Training
  - Field staff
  - Headquarters staff

Annexes: management theory, evaluation process and formats, fact sheets

The work on protected areas has not so far been integrated into an effective regional and local land and resource use planning process. Much work also remains to be done to develop effective integrated conservation and development projects in the Lao protected areas which respond appropriately to the diverse needs and aspirations of local communities while also protecting significant biodiversity values.

The NBCAs remain very generic in purpose. The task of working out more specific objectives (and management classification) remains ahead.

Perceived advantages of the Lao PDR national system plan are:

■ Systematic nation-wide assessment of forest cover, biogeographical zonation and presence of indicator species as the basis for site selection.

■ Emphasis on decentralised responsibility for implementation, with extensive consultation with provinces to seek their approval prior to selection of each site.

Factors which should be considered in assessing the transferability of the Lao approach to other contexts include:

■ It was based on the relatively unusual opportunity to start from scratch. The lack of an inherited system may be attractive – such as in presenting a "clean slate" for application of explicit iterative biogeography-based methods – but it also means there is little institutional experience in balancing the competing interests of conservation and development.

■ There remain difficulties of providing effective central co-ordination and transborder collaboration between provinces and with neighbouring countries.

■ The central co-ordinating agency is restricted to an advisory role, limiting its capacity to guarantee protection of the agreed areas.

■ Implementation to date has been largely dependent on donor assistance, which means that sustainability of the system at national level remains to be tested.

■ The situation of the Lao PDR is rather different from many of its neighbours in that a high proportion of forest cover remains, and population density is still low.

For further information about Lao PDR system planning, contact:

Centre for Protected Areas and Watershed Management, Dep. Forestry, Ministry of Agriculture and Forestry, Vientiane, Lao PDR or IUCN country office, PO Box 4340 (15 Fa Ngum Road), Vientiane, Lao PDR; phone 00856-21-216401, fax 00856-21-216127.

Appendix 4

References cited

AMEND, Stephan and AMEND, Thora, eds (1995) *National parks without people? The South American experience.* IUCN/Parques Nacionales y Conservación Ambiental, No. 5, Quito

BATISSE M. (1997) *Biosphere Reserves: A Challenge for Biodiversity Conservation and Regional Development.* Environment 39(5) 6–15,31–33.

BEDWARD, M., PRESSEY, R.L. and KEITH, D.A. (1992) *A new approach for selecting fully representative reserve networks: addressing efficiency, reserve design and land suitability with an iterative analysis.*Biological Conservation 62: 115–125.

BELBIN, L. (1992) *Environmental representativeness: regional partitioning and reserve selection.* Biological Conservation 66: 223–230.

BERKMÜLLER, Klaus, SOUTHAMMAKOTH, Sangthong and VONGPHET, Vene (1995) *Protected area system planning and management in Lao PDR: status report to mid-1995.* IUCN and Lao-Swedish Forestry Co-operation Program, Forest Resource Conservation Project, Vientiane.

BORRINI-FEYERABEND, Grazia, ed. (1997) *Beyond Fences: Seeking Sustainability in Conservation.* IUCN/Commission on Environmental, Economic and Social Policy, Gland, Switzerland.

CANADA. Canadian Environmental Advisory Council (1991) *A protected areas vision for Canada.* Environment Canada, Ottawa.

CANADA. Department of Canadian Heritage (1995) *Sea to sea to sea: Canada's national marine conservation system plan.* The Department, Ottawa.

CANADA. Environment Canada. Parks Service (1991) *National parks system plan.* Environment Canada, Ottawa.

CANADA. Province of British Columbia (1993) *A protected areas strategy for British Columbia.* Protected Areas Strategy, Victoria.

CAUGHLEY, Graeme and GUNN, Anne (1996) *Conservation biology in theory and practice.* Blackwell, Boston.

CHAPE, Stuart (1996) *Biodiversity conservation, protected areas and the development imperative in Lao PDR: forging the links.* IUCN Lao PDR, Vientiane. Discussion paper no. 1.

CHILD, G. and GRAINGER, J. (1990) *A system plan for protected areas for wildlife conservation and sustainable rural development in Saudi Arabia.* National Commission for Wildlife Conservation and Development, Riyadh.

CNPPA (1996) *Assessing benefits to the economy from protected areas: a summary for decision-makers.* DRAFT, Commission on National Parks and Protected Areas, IUCN, Gland.

DAVEY, Adrian G. (1996a) *National protected area system planning for Pakistan.* Report to Government of Pakistan, IUCN Pakistan and IUCN Commission on National Parks and Protected Areas. Applied Ecology Research Group, University of Canberra.

DAVEY, Adrian G. (1996b) *Strategic issues and directions for a protected area system plan for Zambia.* Report to the Zambian National Parks and Wildlife Service, IUCN Zambia and IUCN Commission on National Parks and Protected Areas. Applied Ecology Research Group, University of Canberra.

DAVEY, Adrian G. (1996c) *A strategy for development of a protected area system plan for Cambodia.* Report to Cambodian Ministry of the Environment, IUCN Cambodia and IUCN Commission on National Parks and Protected Areas. Applied Ecology Research Group, University of Canberra.

FORSTER, Richard R. (1973) *Planning for man and nature in national parks: reconciling perpetuation and use.* IUCN, Morges. IUCN publn n.s. no. 26.

GLOWKA, Lyle, BURHENNE-GUILMIN, Françoise, SYNGE, Hugh, MCNEELY, Jeffrey A. and GÜNDLING, Lothar (1994) *A guide to the Convention on Biological Diversity.* IUCN, Gland. IUCN Environmental Law Centre, Environmental Policy and Law paper no. 30.

GREEN, M.J.B. and PAINE, J.R. (1997). *State of the World's Protected Areas at the End of the Twentieth Century.* Paper Presented at "Protected Areas in the 21st Century: From Islands to Networks" Albany, Australia, 24–29th November 1997.

HAMILTON, Larry, MACRAY, Janet, WORBOYS, Graeme, JONES, Robert and MANSON, Gregor (1996) *Transborder Protected Area Co-operation.* IUCN and Australian Alps National Parks.

HARMON, David, ed. (1994) *Co-ordinating research and management to enhance protected areas.* IUCN, Gland.

HARRISON, Jeremy (1992) *Protected area management guidelines.* Parks 3(2): 22–25.

HART, William J. (1996) *A systems approach to park planning.* IUCN, Morges. IUCN publn n.s. supp. pap no. 4.

IUCN (1978) *Categories, objectives and criteria for protected areas.* Commission in National Parks and Protected Areas, Committee on Criteria and Nomenclature. IUCN, Gland.

IUCN (1992a) *Caracas action plan. Declaration and conclusions of the IVth World Congress on National Parks and Protected Areas, Caracas Venezuela February 1992.* IUCN Programme on Protected Areas / CNPPA, Gland.

IUCN (1992b) *Protected areas of the world.* IUCN, Gland. Four volumes.

IUCN (1994) *Guidelines for protected area management categories.* IUCN Commission on National Parks and Protected Areas with the assistance of the World Conservation Monitoring Centre. IUCN, Gland.

IUCN (1997) *United Nations list of national parks and protected areas 1997.* IUCN, Gland.

KELLEHER, Graeme and KENCHINGTON, Richard (1991) *Guidelines for establishing marine protected areas.* IUCN, Gland.

KEMF, Elizabeth, ed. (1993) *The law of the mother: protecting indigenous peoples in protected areas.* Sierra Club Books, San Francisco.

LUCAS, P.H.C. (1992) *Protected landscapes: a guide for policy-makers and planning.* Chapman and Hall, London.

LUSIGI, Walter ed. (1992) *Managing Protected Areas in Africa: Report from a Workshop on Protected Area Management in Africa, Mweka, Tanzania.* UNESCO World Heritage Fund, Paris, France.

MACKINNON, John, MACKINNON, Kathy, CHILD, Graham and THORSELL, Jim (1986) *Managing protected areas in the tropics.* IUCN, Gland.

MARGULES, C.R., CRESSWELL, I.D. and NICHOLLS, A.O. (1994) *A scientific basis for establishing networks of protected areas.* Pp. 327–350 in: FOREY, P.L., HUMPHRIES, C.J. and VANE-WRIGHT, R.I., eds (1994) *Systematics and conservation evaluation.* Clarendon Press, Oxford.

MARGULES, C.R., NICHOLLS, A.O. and PRESSEY, R.L. (1988) *Selecting networks of reserves to maximise biological diversity.* Biological Conservation 43: 63–76.

McNEELY, Jeffrey, ed. (1993) *Parks for life: report of the IVth World Congress on national parks and protected areas.* IUCN, Gland.

McNEELY, J.A., HARRISON, J. and DINGWALL, P. eds (1994) *Protecting nature: regional reviews of protected areas.* IUCN, Gland.

McNEELY, Jeff and THORSELL, Jim (1991) *Guidelines for preparing protected area system plans.* Parks 2(2): 4–8.

MILLER, K. (1996) *Balancing the scales.* World Resources Institute, Washington.

NELSON, J.G. (1987) *National Parks and protected areas, national conservation strategies and sustainable development.* Geoforum 18(3): 291–319.

PEARSALL, S.H. and WHISTLER, W.A. (1991) *Terrestrial ecosystem mapping for Western Samoa: summary, project report and proposed national parks and reserves plans.* Report to Government of Western Samoa. South Pacific Regional Environment Program and Environment and Policy Institute of East West Centre.

PERES, Carlos A. and TERBORGH, John W. (1995) *Amazonian nature reserves: an analysis of the defensibility status of existing conservation units and design criteria for the future.* Conservation Biology 9 (1):34–36.

POORE, Duncan, ed. (1992) *Guidelines for mountain protected areas.* IUCN, Gland. Protected Area programmes series no. 2.

PRESSEY, R.L., BEDWARD, M. and KEITH, D.A. (1994) *New procedures for reserve selection in New South Wales: maximising the chances of achieving a representative network.* Pp. 351–373 in: FOREY, P.L., HUMPHRIES, C.J. and VANE-WRIGHT, R.I., eds (1994) *Systematics and conservation evaluation.* Clarendon Press, Oxford.

PRESSEY, R.L., HUMPHRIES, C.J., MARGULES, C.R., VANE-WRIGHT, R.I. and WILLIAMS, P.H. (1993) *Beyond opportunism: key principles for systematic reserve selection.* Trends in Ecology and Evolution 8(4): 124–128.

PRESSEEY, R.L. and LOGAN, V.S. (1994) *Level of geographical subdivision and its effects on assessments of reserve coverage: a review of regional studies.* Conservation Biology 8(4): 1037–1046.

REPUBLICA DOMINICANA. DVS (1990) *La diversidad biologica en la Republica Dominicana.* Departamento de Vida Silvestre, Santo Domingo.

RODGERS, W.A. and PANWAR, H.S. (1988) *Planning a wildlife protected area network in India.* FAO, Dehra Dun.

SALTER, R.E. and PHANTHAVONG, B. (1989) *Needs and priorities for a protected area system in Lao PDR.* IUCN and Lao-Swedish Forestry Co-operation Program, Forest Resource Conservation Project, Vientiane.

SCOTT, J.M., DAVIS, F., CSUTI, B., NOSS, R., BUTTERFIELD, B., GROVES, C., ANDERSON, H., CAICCO, S., D'ERCHIA, F., EDWARDS, T.C., ULLIMAN, J. and WRIGHT, R.G. (1993) *Gap analysis: a geographic approach to protection of biological diversity.* Wildlife Monographs No. 123 [suppl. to *J. Wildl. Management* 57(1)].

THEBERGE, John B. (1989) *Guidelines to drawing ecologically sound boundaries for national parks and nature reserves.* Environmental Management 13(6): 695–702.

THORSELL, J., ed. (1990) *Parks on the borderline: experience in trans-frontier conservation.* IUCN, Gland.

UDVARDY, M.D.F. (1975) *A classification of the biogeographical provinces of the world.* IUCN, Gland. Occasional paper no. 18.

UNESCO (1996) *Biosphere Reserves: Seville Strategy and the Strategy Framework of the World Network.* UNESCO, Paris.

VENEZUELA. MARNR (1989) *Marco conceptual del plan del sistema nacional de areas naturales protegidas.* Ministerio del Ambiente y de los Recursos Naturales Renovables, Caracas.

WEST, Patrick C. and BRECHIN, Steven R., eds (1991) *Resident peoples and national parks.* University of Arizona Press, Tucson.

Appendix 5

Contact addresses

WCPA

Protected Areas Programme
IUCN – The World Conservation Union
Rue Mauverney 28, CH-1196 Gland
Switzerland
Tel: 004122 999 0162
Fax: 004122 999 0015
Email: das@hq.iucn.org
http://www.iucn.org/

IUCN Publications

IUCN Publications Services Unit
219c Huntingdon Road
Cambridge, CB3 0DL, UK
Tel: 0044 (0) 1223 277894
Fax: 0044 (0) 1223 277175
Email: iucn-psu@wcmc.org.uk
http://www.iucn.org/

WCMC

World Conservation Monitoring Centre
219 Huntingdon Road
Cambridge, CB3 0DL, UK
Tel: 0044 (0) 1223 277314
Fax: 0044 (0) 1223 277136
Email: info@wcmc.org.uk
http://www.wcmc.org.uk/